Praise for *The Health* *Navigating t*

"*This book cracks the code on how to bring improvements to a part of the hospital that for too long has been literally and figuratively closed to senior leaders. Gerald Biala and Therese Fitzpatrick have created a must-read handbook for any senior executive who hopes to be successful in leading a hospital.*"

–Mark Taylor
President and CEO (retired)
Columbia-St. Mary's Health System

"*The work that is laid out in this book is like a recipe for success in managing the complexities of surgical services. I can speak firsthand to having Gerry and his team assist us in improving our efficiencies within our surgical services department. The most impactful decision made was implementing a PEC structure. Without this structure, all other performance improvement work would not have been successful. I could not recommend this book more highly.*"

–Mandy Richards, MSN, RN, ACNS-BC, CNRN
System Chief Nursing Officer

'The Healthcare Executive's Guide to Navigating the Surgical Suite *is a practical and essential read for graduate students, surgical residents, physicians, and executives alike. Often considered the 'Do Not Enter' area of the hospital, it is nevertheless the engine that pulls the train and is core to an organization's success. An excellent example of shared governance decision-making, it is a practical and contemporary approach to best practices.*"

–Steven A. Fellows, FACHE
Executive Vice President and Chief Operating Officer
Cottage Health

"*This book condenses salient points of information important to those responsible for leading the surgical services department through the ever-changing healthcare environment. It is a must-read for anyone contemplating a surgical services leadership position or as a refresher for those already in the role. It was an interesting and easy read, providing a quick scan of topics important to delivering efficient and effective care in surgical services.*"

–Cynthia D. Sweeney, MSN, RN, CNOR, NEA-BC
Executive Director, The DAISY Foundation

"As the Chief Executive for one of the state's largest specialty surgical groups, with an ambulatory surgery center doing outpatient total joints, I find myself at the intersection of any number of the concepts Biala and Fitzpatrick address in this book. Patients, payers, and evolving surgical science are driving significant changes in our business models and investment decisions. Our surgeons and I have responsibility for determining our ambulatory surgery strategy, including the development of new sites of care while simultaneously optimizing our relationships with affiliate hospitals. I can certainly attest to the complexity of developing relationships where collaboration and competition are in delicate balance. What continues to be constant in surgical practice, however, is the need for surgeons to maximize their productivity, minimize clinical and legal risk, and leverage the talents of a sizable interdisciplinary team to drive clinical outcomes. This book is a valuable resource to these ends."

–David Kanzler
Chief Executive Officer
Hinsdale Orthopedics

"If it seems difficult to get past the sterile barriers and into the unique world of surgery, Biala and Fitzpatrick will succinctly help you understand both surgical culture and operations. Intended for healthcare executives, this book uniquely prepares leaders to ask better questions to both manage and improve surgical efficiency, reliability, and profitability. The insights in this book will shorten your learning curve in surgical services."

–Charles L. Derus, MD
Vice President, Medical Management
Advocate Aurora Good Samaritan Hospital

"An excellent roadmap for a chief nursing officer, as well as a resource that can be referred to over and over again."

–Christine Budzinsky, CNO
AMITA Health Alexian Brothers Medical Center and
AMITA Health St. Alexius Medical Center

"The Healthcare Executive's Guide to Navigating the Surgical Suite unveils the mystery behind highly restricted, locked, double door entry of the surgical sanctum with its own strict dress code in every hospital. Gerald Biala has worked his way up to the present master consultant position starting from the bottom up, like most in the field of perioperative surgery. Biala and Fitzpatrick have done a great job of sharing this enormous experience, otherwise learned by on-the-job training. All eight chapters of the book deal with intricate, discrete, closely related machinations of the operating suites environment, dealing with multiple stakeholders. I am very impressed with the detailed descriptions and methodology of organizing highly trained and accomplished professionals of different backgrounds, each with their independent mind-set, to work together for a common mission and goal. This guide will serve as a must-read treatise for all, dealing with contemporary leadership in this field."

–Vijay K. Maker, MD, FACS, FRCSc
Chairman of Surgery
Division Head General Surgery, Advocate Illinois Masonic Hospital
Professor of Surgery, University of Illinois
Program Director, University of Illinois/Metro Group Hospitals
Residency in General Surgery

THE HEALTHCARE EXECUTIVE'S GUIDE TO

NAVIGATING THE SURGICAL SUITE

A ROADMAP TO THE OR AND PERIOPERATIVE SERVICES

Gerald E. Biala, MSN, RN, CNOR, CSSM

Therese A. Fitzpatrick, PhD, RN, FAAN

Sigma
GLOBAL NURSING
EXCELLENCE

The Sigma Theta Tau International Honor Society of Nursing (Sigma) is a nonprofit organization whose mission is advancing world health and celebrating nursing excellence in scholarship, leadership, and service. Founded in 1922, Sigma has more than 135,000 active members in over 90 countries and territories. Members include practicing nurses, instructors, researchers, policymakers, entrepreneurs, and others. Sigma's more than 530 chapters are located at more than 700 institutions of higher education throughout Armenia, Australia, Botswana, Brazil, Canada, Colombia, England, Ghana, Hong Kong, Japan, Jordan, Kenya, Lebanon, Malawi, Mexico, the Netherlands, Pakistan, Philippines, Portugal, Singapore, South Africa, South Korea, Swaziland, Sweden, Taiwan, Tanzania, Thailand, the United States, and Wales. Learn more at www.sigmanursing.org.

Sigma Theta Tau International
550 West North Street
Indianapolis, IN, USA 46202

To order additional books, buy in bulk, or order for corporate use, contact Sigma Marketplace at 888.654.4968 (US/Canada toll-free) or +1.317.634.8171 (International).

To request a review copy for course adoption, email solutions@sigmamarketplace.org or call 888.654.4968 (US/Canada toll-free) or +1.317.634.8171 (International).

To request author information, or for speaker or other media requests, contact Sigma Marketing at 888.634.7575 (US/Canada toll-free) or +1.317.634.8171 (International).

ISBN: 9781945157820
EPUB ISBN: 9781945157837
PDF ISBN: 9781945157844
MOBI ISBN: 9781945157851

Library of Congress Cataloging-in-Publication data

Names: Biala, Gerald E., 1952- author. | Fitzpatrick, Therese, 1953- author.
    | Sigma Theta Tau International, issuing body.
Title: The healthcare executive's guide to navigating the surgical suite : a
    roadmap to the OR and perioperative services / Gerald E. Biala, Therese A.
    Fitzpatrick.
Description: Indianapolis, IN, USA : Sigma Theta Tau International, [2019] |
    Includes bibliographical references.
Identifiers: LCCN 2018040424| ISBN 9781945157820 (pbk.) | ISBN 9781945157844
    (pdf ebook) | ISBN 9781945157851 (amazon/mobi ebook) | ISBN 9781945157837
    (epub ebook)
Subjects: | MESH: Hospital Administration | Operating Rooms--organization &
    administration | Perioperative Care
Classification: LCC RA971 | NLM WX 159 | DDC 362.11068--dc23 LC record available at
    https://lccn.loc.gov/2018040424

First Printing, 2018

Publisher: Dustin Sullivan
Acquisitions Editor: Emily Hatch
Publications Specialist: Todd Lothery
Cover Designer: TnT Design Inc.
Interior Design/Page Layout: Rebecca Batchelor
Illustrator: Michael Tanamachi

Managing Editor: Carla Hall
Development and Project Editor: Meaghan O'Keeffe
Copy Editor: Erin Geile
Proofreader: Gill Editorial Services
Indexer: Larry Sweazy

DEDICATIONS

This book is dedicated to the men and women of the United States Armed Forces. My first exposure to healthcare was serving in the United States Air Force, where I was inspired to dedicate my career to patient care. The clinical, organizational, and logistics training I received was invaluable to my career in the surgical services.

–Gerald Biala

This book is dedicated to my children, Nina and Andrew Pilacoutas, whose thoughtful opinions and genuine optimism provide confidence that our world will be well cared for by the incredible millennial generation. You teach me something new each time we are together, and I could not be more proud.

–Therese Fitzpatrick

ACKNOWLEDGMENTS

We would like to thank our many dedicated clients and colleagues who have trusted us over many years and provided the insights highlighted in this book. Their thoughtful questions and candor led us to recognize that even the most experienced and skillful executive needed to be armed with additional tools for managing surgical services.

We are especially grateful to Linda Pophal for her hard work, perseverance, and willingness to meet completely unreasonable deadlines.

Sigma's editorial staff has provided unwavering support in this effort. Thank you to Emily Hatch and Carla Hall, who were enormously helpful in providing technical assistance and encouragement throughout our journey.

ABOUT THE AUTHORS

Gerald E. Biala, MSN, RN, CNOR, CSSM, is a Surgical Services Management Consultant and Managing Partner for Precision Consulting Services Inc., a consultancy committed to providing healthcare consultation following a collaborative implementation program model. Its focus is to augment healthcare organizations' ability to attain their strategic goals and operational objectives by providing leaders with deep knowledge and experience in the perioperative services. The primary mission is to provide implementation support. Desired change is achieved by targeted operational involvement in daily management and the application of technological tools to enable this change. Knowledge and experience are leveraged to identify solutions and gain alignment or consensus with senior leadership, surgeons, anesthesiologists, and hospital staff. PCS provides a comprehensive set of services that are tailored to the unique needs of an organization. These services are structured along a flexible range of support levels, from advisory through transitional leadership.

Biala also works for Sullivan Healthcare Consulting as its Senior Vice President of Implementation Services. Sullivan Healthcare Consulting, LLC (SHC), specializes in perioperative, sterile processing, and surgical consulting, as well as implementation and interim management in hospitals of all sizes and types across the United States and Canada. Originally established in 1975, SHC has operated continuously since that time as various corporate entities, including under the umbrella of Johnson & Johnson Consulting and Services from 1995 to 2003. Currently part of the Jackson Healthcare Family of Companies, SHC has a stellar reputation for the provision of cutting-edge assessment and implementation services in the perioperative area.

Biala has over 40 years of healthcare experience focused on care of the surgical patient and related clinical support areas. He has served as the director of surgical services departments in both academic and community settings and was on the faculty of Rush University for several years. He entered the consulting industry working for Ernst & Young as a National Practice Leader for Surgical Services and served as a Principal in its healthcare consulting group, leaving after 5 years to establish a consulting practice focused on the implementation of change. He also served for 5 years as a Senior Vice President for Surgical Care Affiliates, a leader in the outpatient surgery industry. In addition, he is a retired officer with the United States Air Force Reserve.

He has spoken at several professional venues on surgical services governance models and surgical co-management arrangements and has continued his research and publication on the growth and development of operating room specialty team organizational models.

Biala received his MSN from Rush University in Chicago with a focus on nursing care of the patient in the operating room. He received his BSN from DePaul University in Chicago. He currently holds certifications as a certified perioperative nurse and a certified surgical services manager.

Therese A. Fitzpatrick, PhD, RN, FAAN, is Senior Vice President and member of the Performance Improvement Practice at Kaufman Hall Associates in Skokie, Illinois. Kaufman Hall advises hospitals and health systems in the effective management of strategic, financial, and operational performance. Fitzpatrick's practice focuses on assessing clinical and operational performance and developing effective strategies to enhance efficiency and optimize staffing.

Fitzpatrick has over 40 years of healthcare experience spanning operations and policy development in local, regional, and global markets.

Her areas of expertise include strategic management of clinical and administrative services, analytical and financial competencies, labor relations and contract negotiations, and strategic workforce optimization, with a specialty focus in developing clinical staffing algorithms based on advanced mathematical modeling.

Fitzpatrick served as a Principal and Practice Operations Lead for Philips Healthcare, North America. In that role, she provided strategic and analytical support to governments, regional entities, and individual hospitals and health systems in creating sustainable population health solutions and clinical/business performance improvement across the continuum of care.

Her prior positions include Executive Vice President at Assay Healthcare Solutions, a New York-based, investor-backed consulting and analytics firm focused on the use of mathematical optimization modeling in strategic clinical workforce planning and deployment. The company was built around the science of logistics and the adaptation of sophisticated tools and techniques used with great success in a multitude of other industries outside of healthcare.

Fitzpatrick was also a founding partner of The Optimé Group, a self-funded company that provided technology solutions and business process support services that enabled healthcare clients to improve decision-making and optimize critical processes.

She has also served as a Chief Nursing Officer and Chief Operating Officer at both community and academic organizations and served as a Chief Executive Officer of a successful private-equity-owned nurse staffing company.

Fitzpatrick is also an Assistant Clinical Professor at the University of Illinois-Chicago College of Public Health, where she teaches in the graduate Health Systems Science executive program. In addition, she is on faculty at Augusta University's College of Nursing in Augusta, Georgia, where she serves on the advisory board for the Administrative DNP program. Her research interests include workforce productivity, complexity management, systems theory, and healthcare governance.

With Connie Curran, she published *Claiming the Corner Office: Executive Leadership Lessons for Nurses* (Sigma, 2013). Her work has also been featured in a number of administrative journals and at professional meetings. She recently presented the results of research on optimizing nursing human capital at the International Nursing Administration Research meeting, The Royal College of Surgeons Ireland, and the annual meeting of the American Organization of Nurse Executives. Her work on human capital optimization received the Greatest Potential Contribution to Nursing Practice award from the Royal College. She and a colleague at UIC have recently published a chapter in the fourth edition of Huber's *Leadership and Nursing Care Management* focused on financial management.

Fitzpatrick serves on the editorial boards of *Nursing Economics* and *Journal of Nursing Regulation* and on the governance council of Advocate Good Samaritan Hospital. She also serves on the board of directors for Turning Point Community Mental Health Center in Skokie, Illinois, and as Chair of the advisory board for DePaul University's College of Science and Health. She is a recipient of the Baldrige Award.

She received her PhD in urban studies at the University of Wisconsin-Milwaukee. Her research interest is in the creation of community through community planning and architecture. She received her BSN from DePaul University in Chicago along with her MS in nursing administration with a particular focus in human resource management and labor relations. Fitzpatrick also received certification in Negotiating Strategy from Harvard University.

Maggie Ozan Rafferty, DHA, RN, serves as the Chief Experience Officer for Blessing Health System (BHS). Her responsibilities include driving the patient experience agenda for the integrated system located in central Illinois. She is also an adjunct professor in the School of Business and Health Administration at the University of St. Francis in Joliet, Illinois, and in the Health Administration and Doctor of Nursing programs at the University of Nevada, Las Vegas.

Prior to joining BHS, Rafferty held executive positions in operations education, consulting, and management services. She served for 5 years as the first Chief Experience Officer for Dignity Health's Nevada market. She was the Vice President of Operations for the School of Nursing at Rasmussen College. She also served as Vice President at Silver Cross Hospital in New Lenox, Illinois. In this role she was a member of the executive team, which championed the hospital's turnaround to become a Thomson 100 Top Hospital.

During her DHA program, Rafferty became interested in the topic of globalization of health services and the concept of international travel for healthcare. Her area of research is medical tourism, and her dissertation evaluated the online narratives of health travelers to Turkey. The findings from her dissertation were published in the *Journal of Internet Research*. She has also authored additional articles on driving exceptional patient experiences and has presented at numerous conferences in the US and overseas.

Rafferty holds a master's degree in health administration from Governors State University, an MBA from the University of Chicago's Booth School of Business, and a DHA from Central Michigan University. She is a member of numerous professional organizations.

TABLE OF CONTENTS

FOREWORD

As a healthcare executive for 41 years—including President of Advocate Good Samaritan Hospital and senior leader of its journey to excellence over the past 15 years—it is my privilege and pleasure to write the foreword for this extraordinarily useful and well-written guide. The book contains specific, immediately applicable principles and practices of how to achieve and sustain outstanding outcomes in the surgical suite.

The Healthcare Executive's Guide to Navigating the Surgical Suite could not be timelier, as the healthcare industry is clearly entering an era of massive, disruptive change. Legacy hospitals are increasingly under attack by more nimble competitors that are building ambulatory surgery centers, office-based GI centers, urgent care centers, and freestanding imaging centers within our traditional markets.

As if this reality were not challenging enough, reimbursement from government and commercial payers has flatlined or even begun to decline in many markets across the United States. At the same time, growth of high-deductible commercial health plans has caused patients to begin acting like consumers who are genuinely interested in the price—especially the out-of-pocket costs—of their care.

A perfect storm seems to be upon us. Gerald Biala and Therese Fitzpatrick have written a guide to help leaders of surgical services not just weather the storm but successfully navigate it to position their hospital for continued success.

It is difficult to be a successful hospital without a strong, growing surgery department. And, to be successful within perioperative services, surgery leaders must proactively and skillfully partner with surgeons and anesthesiologists in managing labor, room utilization, supplies, and surgical implant expenses. The role of the surgery leader is indisputably one of the most challenging and complex jobs in healthcare management.

The authors have written an easily readable yet detailed roadmap on how to run a more efficient, affordable, and high-reliability operating room. At the end of each chapter, the authors also provide a concise and highly useful summary titled Executive Leadership Lessons. These summaries, which distill lessons learned from the authors' many years of operating room experience, enable the reader to easily understand and synthesize the most important takeaways from the material. New directors of perioperative services, or even seasoned veterans, will find this book to be an invaluable resource for identifying best practices and taking their organization to an even higher level of performance.

While much of the content of this guide is specifically directed toward attainment of clinical, patient safety, operational, and financial excellence within the surgical suite, the lessons are applicable to many aspects of a hospital's successful operation.

Even for surgical suites that have historically operated profitably with good patient outcomes, success is never final. The realities of the new market require surgery leaders to continually redesign services to further reduce waste and avoidable cost, provide a retail-like experience for patients, and preserve the hospital's operating and procedure rooms as the preferred practice sites for surgeons.

I became familiar with many of the principles in *The Healthcare Executive's Guide to Navigating the Surgical Suite* during previous work with Therese Fitzpatrick. I first met her in 2007, when Advocate Good Samaritan Hospital retained her as a consultant to help implement a staffing optimization model for nursing services. I came to know

Therese as an extremely bright, data-driven, analytical, and compassionate colleague. She had a knack for making people around her feel comfortable and trusting. She also had an ability to explain her ideas and approaches in ways that generated understanding and support from our nurses.

Following the conclusion of this successful engagement, I prevailed upon Therese to join our governing council, a role she served with distinction—including 3 years as board chair. Along the way, we became good friends.

Both as consultant to the hospital and then later as board chair of the governing council, Therese supported and helped guide Advocate Good Samaritan Hospital on its journey to performance excellence. By applying many of the principles clearly explained in this book, Good Samaritan Hospital received the prestigious Malcolm Baldrige National Quality Award in 2010. Since then, Truven Analytics, Healthgrades, Becker's, CMS, and other organizations have continued to recognize Good Samaritan for its superior clinical outcomes. Therese also supported our successful efforts to become a Magnet hospital for nursing excellence.

I anticipate that even veteran leaders of perioperative services will find *The Healthcare Executive's Guide to Navigating the Surgical Suite* to be a useful companion for success in navigating the challenging healthcare environment of today and tomorrow.

–David S. Fox
Former President (2003–2018)
Advocate Good Samaritan Hospital

INTRODUCTION

Congratulations—you did it! You have achieved that coveted position in the C-suite. As a new executive in perioperative services, your learning curve will be steep and rapid. You are no doubt consumed with learning the rules of engagement, setting strategy, and familiarizing yourself with the unique needs of your varied constituents. You will need to cultivate relationships with the members of the board of directors, and you will become familiar with every line on the profit and loss statement.

The operating room (and the clinical areas that support surgical services) is the area of the organization that is often most isolated from general operations—and therefore shrouded in mystery. Yet this department represents a sizable portion of the hospital's revenue, as well as capital expense. Surgeon efficiency is inextricably tied to hospital systems and processes; when things go awry—such as a scheduling delay or unavailability of specialized equipment—the downstream effects can be significant.

Tensions may run high in this clinical area, where patients are completely dependent on physicians and nurses for life support and to keep them from harm. Surgical services are among the most high-risk healthcare specialties, making teamwork and effective communication critical. Every aspect of care delivery, from the physical environment to piped-in gases, dress, infection control, and the movement of patients, must be executed in complete lockstep. Missteps can lead to catastrophic results.

Let Us Be Your Guides

The Healthcare Executive's Guide to Navigating the Surgical Suite provides a glimpse into the complex surgical service environment, covering contemporary market realities, business challenges, clinical and operational complexities, and labor requirements.

Throughout our leadership and consulting careers, we have had the opportunity to familiarize countless new executives with the strategic and operational environment of the surgical service business line. These colleagues and client executives have provided rich feedback on their early learning priorities, challenges to their emerging executive role related to surgical services, and areas of leadership where they felt ill-prepared (spoiler alert: strategic physician relationships). Graciously offering their perspectives and experiences as new leaders, these executives have responded to a myriad of questions, such as "What do you wish you knew about surgical services prior to attending your first OR Governance Committee breakfast or before walking into a town hall meeting with the operating room staff? What would have helped you to confidently negotiate that first payer contract? If you could provide guidance to the new C-suite executive, what does that individual need to know about surgical services to be successful?"

Although we cannot provide a specific answer for every daunting question facing the new executive, over the course of these pages we do hope to provide insight into the rapidly evolving surgical service specialty. Topics include the market for these services, the changing expectations of the consumer, effective governance strategies, the balance of strategic and operational objectives, and creative business and labor models.

This book is intended to point new leaders toward the most pressing executive issues in the strategic leadership of surgical services. It addresses pitfalls and vulnerabilities and evolving market and payer challenges. It does so while offering examples of strategic approaches that may be of benefit in the new executive's situation. It also provides help with difficult conversations with diverse constituencies. Knowing what to expect, how to frame the problem, and best practices and successful strategies will significantly increase your confidence and negotiating position, whether with payers, providers, or innovative new business partners.

Chapter 1 provides an overview of the competitive landscape and the market forces uniquely impacting surgical services, including payer and regulator practices and bundled payment schemes with the goal of minimizing reimbursement. The demographics of the labor force play a significant role in both current staffing and the development of succession plans for leaders as a disproportionate share of the surgical nursing workforce is poised to retire.

Chapters 2 and 3 focus on effective governance and leadership structures, which are increasingly predicated on a shared, interdisciplinary decision-making model. Balancing the goals and objectives of the varied constituents, including surgeons, anesthesiologists, nurses, and others with the organization's overall strategic objectives, requires a leadership structure rarely seen in the rest of the organization. Roles and responsibilities must be clearly described and accountability explicitly defined.

Chapter 4 offers instruction on creating and monitoring the complex revenue and expense budgets for surgical services. The department is typically composed of a number of cost centers including ambulatory surgery, preoperative test and holding, post-anesthesia recovery, and sterile processing to name a few. Understanding and predicting case volume are both an art and a science with a significant impact on the bottom line. Equipment and supply management requires an effective charge capture system to both manage waste but, more importantly, provide data to understand procedure costs as an important component of negotiating realistic contracts with payers.

Chapter 5 continues the performance conversation with a focus on performance metrics and the means to regularly monitor financial, process, and clinical outcomes. Given the complexity of the multiple constituents who prioritize efficiency and cost effectiveness, accurate monitoring of utilization by specialty will be an important consideration.

Chapters 6 and 7 address the human capital relationships within surgical services. The evolving market is creating the opportunity for innovative partnerships and employment or affiliate relationships with both surgeons and anesthesiologists. In many parts of the country, hospitals are experiencing the end of single or small-group practices. Not unlike the aging nursing staff, boomer-aged physicians are increasingly considering employment relations with hospitals and local or even national practices to mitigate risk and ease administrative burden. Meanwhile, clinical staff are increasingly looking to professional, interdisciplinary practice models predicated on shared and transparent decision-making.

Chapter 8 covers trends in medical tourism, along with other significant trends. While the medical tourism phenomenon was once centered on international travel to perform various elective procedures—from open heart surgery and total joint replacement to cosmetic surgeries—a growing number of employers and insurance companies are seeking out organizations that are successfully demonstrating value—that is, exceptional clinical outcomes, including reduced lengths of stay, at a reasonable cost. These value-driven hospitals may be in the next town or quite literally across the country. In addition to managing the surgical care of these patients, hospital administrators are bundling in travel expenses as well.

At the end of each chapter, you will find "Executive Leadership Lessons" to highlight the information most critical to your success.

We heard from a number of new executive leaders who expressed a desire to become familiar, at an accelerated pace, with the most pressing contemporary issues within surgical services. We hope *The Healthcare Executive's Guide to Navigating the Surgical Suite* provides guidance as you navigate the management world of surgical services and offers creative solutions to the unique challenges you will come across as you lead this important and strategic business line.

–Gerald E. Biala, MSN, RN, CNOR, CSSM
–Therese A. Fitzpatrick, PhD, RN, FAAN

UNIQUE CHALLENGES IN SURGICAL SERVICES

Serving as the leader of surgical services within an organization can be a daunting endeavor for a new executive. Unless they have actually worked at an operating room (OR) table as a surgeon or surgical nurse or managed a surgical product line, most new executive leaders lack an operational frame of reference for the unique concerns and challenges present in the contemporary OR's dynamic environment. The dress is different, the language unique, and the management nuanced. Operating rooms have their own supply chain, scheduling and billing systems, and procedure codes. What can be touched or where one can safely tread is closely monitored.

Once referred to as "the workshop" of the hospital, with all of its tools and gadgets, the OR has rapidly evolved into a high-tech robotic center. Staying current with the ever-evolving clinical evidence on everything from safe patient positioning to the use of sophisticated technologies requires constant practitioner vigilance. Thousands of pages of federal and state regulations, along with various professional association practice guidelines, govern everything from cleaning protocols to physician preceptorships. Well-educated physician and nurse practitioners, emerging from the finest sites of higher learning, require thousands of additional hours of training to be judged proficient in the surgical arts. The fact that operating theatres are by necessity isolated from the rest of hospital operations makes it increasingly difficult for an executive to understand and experience this very different world.

In the past, it was not uncommon for surgical service operations to be the bastion of an elite group of physicians who operated behind closed doors, controlled the granting of practice privileges to colleagues, and determined everything from professional standards of behavior to who would receive preferential time on the OR schedule.

However, the importance of the operating room to the overall success of a healthcare organization has cast a new light—a very bright spotlight—on operating rooms. It is of critical importance for the new executive to gain an immediate understanding of complex OR operations. While simultaneously providing the greatest contribution of total revenue for the average hospital, the OR represents the location of greatest legal and patient-safety risk and the largest investment in physical assets and materials.

Additionally, the rapidly evolving payment landscape now includes innovative provider models affecting ORs and once-unthought-of partnerships. Surgeons can now be competitors and collaborators simultaneously as they develop their own surgical centers. Revolutionary technology is blurring the traditional boundaries of radiology, cardiology, and surgery. The new executive may be rapidly immersed in conversations about building or buying ambulatory centers, recruiting a new surgeon in a technology-intense specialty, or mediating block scheduling conflicts. Such topics rarely, if ever, emerge in other areas of hospital operations.

A SYSTEMS APPROACH

The "operating room" was once the label for actual operating suites and all departmental activities related to the management of ORs, including finance, supply chain, materials management, scheduling, and more. Organizations now recognize that effective management of this complex operation requires a systems approach, both to improve the way a patient experiences a surgical procedure and to align practitioners in the creation of effective and efficient processes. Increased payer interest in this most-costly aspect of healthcare also has fueled the new approach.

Industry process improvement efforts have confirmed the benefit of subsystem alignment as a precursor to system optimization. Once separate silos of care must now function in complete synchronicity for care to be safe, cost-effective, and efficient. Navigating a patient through a surgical event requires the systemic efficiency of the following processes: scheduling in the physician's office; preoperative testing and anesthesia assessment; the arrival and check-in processes; pre-procedure holding; the surgical procedure itself; post-anesthesia recovery; and discharge and post-procedure follow-up. Optimizing any one of these processes does not necessarily improve the entire experience for either the patient or the provider.

As a result, formerly disparate departments or functions typically are now referred to as Perioperative Services or Surgical Services. This name change suggests more than a simple refresh of signage. Driven by contemporary payment structures, optimization of processes and labor across the entire surgical event is required. Additionally, competition is playing a major role. Hospitals are now competing with a growing number of alternate sites for delivery of surgical services, including surgeon offices, ambulatory surgery centers, and even clinics in the local mall. Each of these sites advertises the fact that procedures can be performed cheaper, quicker, and with great convenience. Customers are responding.

The term *surgical services* is used in this text to refer to the surgical product line and the fully integrated system of surgical care, including sites of care (inpatient and outpatient) and their strategic, operational, management, and business processes. When referring to the actual suite where the procedure is performed, the term *operating room* is used.

SURGICAL SERVICES AND THE TRANSFORMATIVE CHANGES IN HEALTHCARE

The next sections describe four major forces that are transforming healthcare in surgical services and beyond, and the response required of surgical services leadership.

Changing Payment Structures for Surgical Care

Highsted and Peters report that "in a financially healthy hospital, surgery generates up to 65% of contribution margin" (2017, para. 2). This suggests that any reluctance to prioritize the efficiency and effectiveness of all aspects of surgical services places the organization and the executive at significant risk. The Centers for Medicare & Medicaid Services (CMS) just released final guidance on mandated episode or bundled payment programs for both joint replacements and cardiac rehabilitation (2017). Despite cancelling mandatory participation in the bundles, CMS continues to believe that bundled payments offer opportunities to improve quality and care coordination while lowering spending. CMS is leaving the door open for voluntary efforts by providers to create less expensive models that offer value and accessibility. Although this particular approach to incentive payment has been suspended (possibly temporarily) by the government, it is clear that the payment environment is rapidly moving to a value-based model. Executives must expect payer reimbursement methodologies that incentivize the delivery of care in less expensive settings, and through less expensive means, with significant emphasis on value and outcomes.

Simply put, as the most expensive operation within most organizations, and the one generating the highest contribution to an organization's overall strategic and financial health, surgical services will continue to find itself under the greatest pressure to cut costs. This makes it a target for disruption as payment strategies evolve. Porter and Kaplan (2016) in the *Harvard Business Review* discuss two likely payment alternatives in the evolution toward value-based reimbursement: *capitation* and *bundled payments*. Each has significant impact on the provision of surgical services.

With *capitation,* the organization receives a fixed payment per year per covered life and must meet all care needs of that population, including required surgical procedures. With the *bundled payment* system, by contrast, providers are paid a set rate for the entire care episode for a certain diagnosis or procedure, such as joint replacement, cardiac surgery, or congestive heart failure. Within this payment, the organization must provide all tests, procedures, devices, and medications.

The authors do not expect a single payment approach in the short term but do foresee plenty of payer-driven experimentation with unique market and geographic nuances. The impact to surgical services likely will be significant, as the total cost of a surgical procedure and the often-lengthy recovery will consume an inordinate percentage of that payment. This phenomenon is accelerating the development of innovative models in surgical services to efficiently manage the episode of care across the entire system, including preoperative preparation, choice of implantable device, and trajectory of postoperative recovery.

The challenge for many legacy hospitals is a lack of agility to make expeditious changes to care models, including development of the most cost-effective venue for care. Disruptive provider models that compete on both cost and convenience threaten expensive, overhead-laden operating rooms. Where community hospitals once competed with other hospitals in town, now surgeon- or investor-owned surgical centers—with considerable ability to provide excellent care at less expense and greater convenience—challenge hospitals to an entirely different scale of operations. In fact, future competition may come from investor-owned facilities or hospitals nationwide or across the globe in the form of domestic or global medical tourism.

The Evolving Market for Surgical Care

As if cost pressures from government and private payers were not challenging enough, traditional market forces governing healthcare are experiencing sea changes as well. The notion that healthcare is local is being challenged from a number of perspectives. Hospitals historically have defined their market based on local demographics. Patient proximity, coupled with aggressive marketing of a skilled team of surgical experts and the most cutting-edge technology, was assumed to be enough to recruit profitable surgical cases to the organization. A stable base of primary care practitioners helped to ensure the pipeline of surgical cases through well-established referral patterns.

While this served hospitals well prior to the advent of value-based shopping for surgical services, Slotkin, Ross, Coleman, and Ryu (2017) suggest that the traditional approach for defining a market is now experiencing significant disruption. Tired of raising insurance costs and opaque quality and clinical outcomes data, large employers like Lowe's, Walmart, GE, and Boeing are setting the quality criteria for a successful surgical outcome at a price they are willing to pay and are negotiating directly with providers to obtain such surgical care for employees irrespective of provider location. This means that a Boeing employee living and working in Chicago's corporate office may be directed to a hospital in Ohio or Seattle for a hip replacement or cardiac procedure.

The majority of surgical procedures performed annually are considered elective or *semi-elective* (clinically necessary but not emergent) and hence, can be "shopped" by employers. Employers nationwide are partnering with payers, payer intermediaries, and business coalitions to identify providers of surgical care that meet specific quality and cost standards. In order to be considered for participation in this type of network, surgical care providers will need to demonstrate value in the purest economic terms—what outcomes can be guaranteed at what cost.

For the hospital looking to participate as a destination provider, the implications are significant. Systems and processes must be reengineered, workflows redesigned, best practices implemented across all practitioner groups, and all unnecessary clinical variation removed. The data and analytical requirements will involve significant investment to provide continuous evidence of value. Next-generation scorecards and performance metrics will provide the evidence that care that heretofore was considered aspirational has indeed become "hardwired" into the organization.

Evolving Relationships With Surgeons: Competitor or Collaborator

The growth of ambulatory centers has been meteoric given new payment approaches, advances in technology, and biopharmaceuticals, which have radically lessened the need for traditional inpatient surgical care. For the most part, surgeons continue to direct cases to a preferred hospital and a preferred level or location for care, whether inpatient or ambulatory. The emergence of surgeons as business owners should not come as a surprise. Whether surgeons are primary owner-investors or partners with a growing number of ambulatory surgery center (ASC) management companies, acute care hospitals increasingly are finding themselves in the thorny position of competing with their referring surgeons for surgical business.

Reporting in *Becker's ASC Review*, Dyrda (2013) notes that between 2001 and 2011, the number of ASC operating rooms doubled in the US, and by 2011, 60% of all hospitals had an ASC within 5 minutes of the hospital. ASCs are big business. In 2011, Medicare made $3.5 billion in payments to ASCs (Dyrda, 2013). This competitive threat for hospitals will only escalate with the continued evolution of minimally invasive surgical techniques, pain management approaches, and non-acute venues for recovery and rehabilitation, including home care and home therapies.

Hospitals were once able to balance the number of highly profitable, less complex cases covered by surgical services with those patients whose multiple comorbidities, lengthy inpatient stays, and overall high resource utilization resulted in lower profitability. With the growth of

ASCs, profitable surgical cases increasingly are diverted from acute care hospitals to ASCs that can achieve clinical outcomes that rival or exceed hospital surgical programs for much lower cost.

UNIQUE LABOR CHALLENGES IN THE OR

In addition to the disruptive payment, market, and competitive forces described here, the new executive faces unique labor challenges with surgical service programs, which threaten the long-term financial health of the organization. While there has been a surge in healthcare hiring, healthcare employees continue to represent a steady 7.3% of U.S. workers (Daly, 2016). According to the Bureau of Labor Statistics (BLS), union members across sectors of the economy represent roughly 11% of the overall workforce (2017).

The American Federation of State, County and Municipal Employees (AFSCME)—United Nurses of America reported that the issues that typically drive organizing efforts among nurses include mandatory shifts, poorly constructed and implemented overtime and on-call policies, and deteriorating relationships with physicians (Holleran, 2001). All of these triggers are prominent in the operating room. Coupled with the administrative isolation of the department, they represent a potential area of smoldering discontent for surgical services. The union reports that nurses in a number of states are lobbying for legislation to end the practice of mandatory overtime. This practice has increased in operating rooms across the country as hospitals attempt to create more flexible schedules to accommodate surgeons and patients.

Personnel management challenges are on a collision course with the unique demographic threats facing surgical services. A 2013 national study of nurses conducted by AMN Healthcare found that 12% of the total nursing workforce is concentrated in the perioperative areas, specifically the operating room and post anesthesia. Patterson, in *OR Manager* (2012), noted that almost 60% of surgical service managers who responded to a survey reported current difficulty filling RN and technician positions. A larger 68% predicted significant difficulty during the next 5 years.

AN OR NURSING SHORTAGE LOOMS

Buerhaus, Staiger, and Auerbach (2000) point to the fact that graduates of nursing diploma programs have concentrated in greatest numbers in the operating room because these programs offered greater exposure and experience in surgical nursing than baccalaureate programs. The shift away from diploma programs means that younger, college-educated nursing students in the late 1970s and through the 1980s were less likely to have been exposed to operating room experiences than in earlier decades. As a large group of expert OR nurses approach retirement, surgical departments are facing a precipitous need for new nurses that will require a lengthy amount of time and resources in order to develop skills and proficiency in the care of surgical patients.

SURGICAL SERVICES AT THE EPICENTER OF HEALTHCARE DISRUPTION

Healthcare is facing disruptive forces beyond any experienced before, and Kaufman (2018) notes that disruption will be faster, bigger, and broader in 2018 and beyond. Creative and well-capitalized industries (such as the technological industry) without a historic presence in healthcare are entering the business, using their experience to redefine and set the standard for the level of service in a customized, immediate world.

Grube (2018) suggests that numerous parallels exist between the retail industry and healthcare. Both are beset by converging forces, including large-scale disruptive competitors, intense pricing pressures, and a need to optimize efficiencies. Healthcare, much like retail, is experiencing a significant decline in revenue as disruptive models from some unlikely sources compete with traditional approaches.

Amid this intense pressure to provide value at lower costs, hospital executives face significant pressure to more effectively and efficiently manage their surgical operations. Labor is scarce and regulatory requirements mounting.

For new executives, the surgical service learning curve is steep, with significant financial and operating risk if they fail to address challenges with thoughtful expedience. The following chapters will provide insight into best practices, shorten the learning curve, and stoke creativity as new executives both prepare surgical services for seismic change and lead the business line through such change.

REFERENCES

AMN Healthcare. (2013). *2013 survey of registered nurses: Generation gap grows as healthcare transforms.* Retrieved from https://www.amnhealthcare.com/uploaded-Files/MainSite/Content/Healthcare_Industry_Insights/Industry_Research/2013_RNSurvey.pdf

Buerhaus, P. I., Staiger, D. O., & Auerbach, D. I. (2000). Why are shortages of hospital RNs concentrated in specialty care units? *Nursing Economics, 18*(3), 111–116. Retrieved from https://www.nurses.com/doc/why-are-shortages-of-hospital-rns-concentrate-0001

Bureau of Labor Statistics (BLS). (2017). *Economic news release: Union members summary.* Retrieved from https://www.bls.gov/news.release/union2.nr0.htm

Centers for Medicare & Medicaid Services (CMS). (2017). *CMS finalizes changes to the Comprehensive Care for Joint Replacement Model, cancels Episode Payment Models and Cardiac Rehabilitation Incentive Payment Model.* [Press release.] Retrieved from https://www.cms.gov/Newsroom/MediaReleaseDatabase/Press-releases/2017-Press-releases-items/2017-11-30.html

Daly, R. (2016). Unionization surges in healthcare. *Healthcare Finance Management Association newsletter.* Retrieved from https://www.hfma.org/Content.aspx?id=46614

Dyrda, L. (2013, October 7). 100 surgery center benchmarks & statistics to know. *Becker's ASC Review.* Retrieved from https://www.beckersasc.com/lists/100-surgery-center-benchmarks-statistics-to-know.html

Grube, M. (2018, January 11). The store is not dead, but the status quo is. *Kaufman Hall.* Retrieved from https://www.kaufmanhall.com/resources/store-not-dead-status-quo?mkt_tok=eyJpIjoiWXprd1l6STRPR0psT1dVMCIsInQiOi-JZSE9NMkxiSEtBbmp2ZHJINGlMUEg0Z1RFWU0xTFgwbVRvRXUwW m1WVGh5Qkl5YThIR0Fwb3A0R3JndGYzNzY1SkJtNG1ka2NlQnZwaVJk-WFByXC9nXC8zN1JVeXZLaVh0WjdtVkzTE5kZjFLYWZmalUyM3ZWV-lJLZ2oxamluelpBIn0%3D

Highsted, B., & Peters, J. (2017, October 9). Q. What single strategy will drive the bulk of OR growth in the next 10 years? A. 360° engagement. *Becker's Hospital Review.* Retrieved from https://www.beckershospitalreview.com/patient-engagement/q-what-single-strategy-will-drive-the-bulk-of-or-growth-in-the-next-10-years-a-360-engagement.html?tmpl=component&print=1&layout=default

Holleran, S. E. (2001, May/June). What do nurses want? *AFSCME Works Magazine.* Retrieved from https://www.afscme.org/news/publications/newsletters/works/mayjune-2001/what-do-nurses-want

Kaufman, K. (2018, January). Faster, bigger, and broader: Healthcare disruption in 2018. *HFM Magazine.* Retrieved from https://www.hfma.org/Content.aspx?id=57409

Patterson, P. (2012). Who will replace retiring perioperative nurses? *OR Manager, 28*(12). Retrieved from www.ormanager.com

Porter, M. E., & Kaplan, R. S. (2016). How to pay for health care. *Harvard Business Review*. Retrieved from https://hbr.org/2016/07/how-to-pay-for-health-care

Slotkin, J. R., Ross, O. A., Coleman, R., & Ryu, J. (2017). Why GE, Boeing, Lowe's, and Walmart are directly buying health care for employees. *Harvard Business Review*. Retrieved from https://hbr.org/2017/06/why-ge-boeing-lowes-and-walmart-are-directly-buying-health-care-for-employees

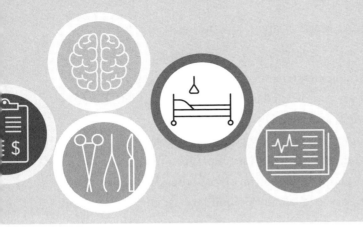

2

GOVERNANCE AND MANAGING RESOURCES

CASE STUDY

Memorial is a 400-bed community acute care hospital with 12 operating rooms. Although the hospital is not currently a member of a larger system, the board is considering a merger with a neighboring hospital. They recognize that efficient operations and a strong balance sheet will be critical to a successful deal. Memorial's surgical revenue has been declining for the past 2 years despite the fact that the facilities and equipment are state-of-the-art. In addition, the department operating expenses have grown, and attempts to reduce supply costs have been met with significant resistance. Staff and surgeons alike have expressed frustration with scheduling inefficiencies, staffing, and insufficient anesthesia coverage. Department leaders feel they do not have the power to make improvements. The current OR committee is chaired by the chief of surgery, reporting to the medical executive committee. The chair of anesthesia and the OR nursing director are members of the committee. The hospital's chief operating officer has expressed concern that the surgeon's interests may not align with the hospital's strategic plan.

It is no secret that the management of a healthcare organization is becoming increasingly complex. Disruptive payment models, significant staffing shortages, and a rapidly changing competitive landscape in which former competitors are now becoming partners suggests a necessary evolution in operational leadership. Once the bastion of physicians with the peripheral involvement of other disciplines, these new-world surgical service challenges require robust conversation and the varied and diverse perspectives of experts from across the enterprise: nurses, finance, marketing, and strategy.

Surgical services' significance to the balance sheet requires close alignment with the organization's strategic planning process as well. Mergers, physician practice acquisitions, innovative partnerships, and the creation of alternate sites of care require surgical services to work closely in tandem with the hospital's strategic planning process.

Experience has shown that shared decision-making among multi-disciplinary groups is a best practice in providing excellent patient care. In surgical services, establishing a well-functioning, multidisciplinary shared decision-making body for managing resources in providing care not only helps to enhance the patient experience, but engages employees as well (Blasco, 2013; OR Manager, Inc., 2007).

There have been many models of governance used to manage groups of employees, including autocratic, hierarchal, and the use of medical staff and hospital committees. However, as the contemporary evidence is demonstrating, none are as effective in building teamwork, productive communication, and mutual respect for all members of the team—and most importantly, improved clinical outcomes—as shared decision-making.

AUTOCRATIC AND HIERARCHICAL GOVERNANCE MODELS

These models typically occur where the chairman of surgery, the chief nursing officer, or the department director wields the power and decision-making. Even when they may seek input from others, they're using an autocratic, or hierarchical, approach to decision-making. This model is generally viewed as outdated, as employee collaboration and input have been shown to result in better outcomes.

There is some support for this model, particularly in high-risk industries that have little room for error. However, this "my way or the highway" approach is least favored among employees, who increasingly want to have input and influence regarding their own work and the outcomes of the organizations they work for. In healthcare, that input is often sought through the committee approach to management.

COMMITTEE GOVERNANCE MODELS

The use of an operating room (OR) committee structure is commonplace in healthcare organizations. This committee generally includes a group of surgeons, anesthesiologists, and nursing directors and managers. It is usually a committee of the medical staff, where physician members are appointed from the medical staff and given the responsibility for oversight of care in the operating room areas. Hospital leaders may sit on the committee but often are not given voting power.

In this structure, decisions are often made without the benefit of hospital administration or nursing services participation and without the alignment of hospital resources. Consequently, many organizations report that their OR committees are not making the decisions needed or implementing needed performance improvement. There typically are larger numbers of surgeons serving on these committees with widely divergent views on managing an operating room, and they often are focused on making decisions that benefit their individual practice, with little consideration given to the organization's strategic goals. Professional respect and the need to maintain collaborative relationships often interfere with tackling the most significant problems involving surgeons. This leads to slow progress and decreased attendance as frustration grows (Heiser, 2013).

Newer approaches to governance include forming a committee that reports directly to administration, which becomes the executive governing body with responsibility and authority to function as a "one-stop" decision-making body for managing department operations and use of resources. There are two basic types of models developing in the industry for these administrative committees: the perioperative executive committee (PEC) with a surgeon advisory group (SAG) or a perioperative governance council (PGC).

The Perioperative Executive Committee (PEC) and the Surgeon Advisory Group (SAG)

The PEC is typically a small body consisting of the department director, the medical directors of surgery and anesthesia, and the senior administrator for perioperative services (VP, CNO, or COO). Additional ad hoc members may include the CEO/COO, CMO, CNO, VP for Strategy, and CFO. These ad hoc members may be critical at times because the PEC sets operational plans and makes decisions that are dependent on system strategy and operations that report to these other senior leaders.

Often it is helpful to have the CEO, COO, or CMO attend the PEC meetings to ensure coordination and successful start-up. This smaller body meets frequently to:

- Manage daily department operations

- Resolve conflicts

- Develop and enforce policy and procedures or guidelines

- Direct performance-improvement projects

- Set targeted utilization levels

- Review key performance measures

- Perform budget planning

The SAG consists of members from the surgical community representing all surgical specialties. Members do not need to hold positions as chairs or chiefs of their departments, but they must be:

- Dedicated to the success of the organization (most often demonstrated as performing the majority of their surgical cases at the hospital).

- Motivated to be part of the management process. Surgeon education, training, and development are entirely clinically focused. They are not exposed to the management process and will need to learn how to be effective on a management team. Some surgeons are not tolerant of this process and should not be selected to serve on management committees.

- Most importantly, surgeons selected should be respected by the surgeon community and influential with their peers.

The PEC relies on the SAG for input on:

- Surgical specialty development

- Review of policy and procedures or guidelines for use of perioperative resources

- Input on daily operations

19

The typical SAG meeting agenda generally consists of two main areas of focus: roundtable feedback from surgeons, and discussions related to key performance-improvement initiatives and activities. The roundtable process provides an open forum for feedback on the functions of the department and concerns for patient care. The department's annual operating plan and key performance measures are reviewed, along with the progress and recommendations for modifying processes or systems for performance improvement.

SAG members are expected to assist in implementation of new programs, policies, and procedures. Although it is important to gain consensus on operational management, the PEC does not give up its authority. The SAG is typically an advisory body, not an approving body. Figures 2.1 and 2.2 outline a sample perioperative executive committee charter and a surgeon advisory group charter, respectively.

Perioperative Executive Committee
CHARTER

NAME:	Perioperative Executive Committee (PEC)
INITIATED DATE:	(Insert)
CHARTER REVIEW:	Quarterly or as needed.
PURPOSE:	This operational committee will have day-to-day responsibility and accountability for the management of resources and overall operations of the Surgical Services, the Ambulatory Surgical Center, and Endoscopy Services. Key responsibilities are to enforce policies, resolve conflicts, and act as the executives of the surgery program maintaining alignment with the organization's strategic plan.
MEETING FREQUENCY:	Every two weeks, or as deemed necessary by the members.

FIGURE 2.1 Sample PEC Charter

REPORTS TO:	CEO
MEMBERSHIP (INCLUDE TITLE AND CREDENTIALS):	Medical Director of Surgical Services
	Medical Directors, Anesthesia
	VP, Clinical Operations
	Director of Patient Care Surgical Services
	Director of Patient Care Perioperative Services
	Ad Hoc Members (i.e., CEO, COO, CMO, CNO, Director PI & Strategy, CFO, Service Chiefs/Medical Directors, Managers or directors and other units/departments)
Chair:	Director of Patient Care Surgical Services
Advisor/Executive Sponsor:	CMO
STATEMENT OF RESPONSIBILITIES:	**Function**
	Define and monitor a surgical services strategic plan that targets services and surgeons for growth consistent with the hospital's overall strategic plan and achieving the highest quality of care.
	Develop an annual department operating plan with clear objectives, initiatives, and coordinated plans for the implementation of change, and expect accountability from each member for agreed-upon actions.
	Provide a safe and efficient environment with optimal anesthesia personnel, nursing and support staff, and equipment to provide the best outcome.
	Promote an environment for all staff and physicians conducive to professional growth and highest levels of satisfaction.
	Ensure excellent and proactive communication regarding changes to roles, responsibilities, expectations, policies, and procedures.
	Review, recommend, or endorse all operational policies that involve surgical services. Create and set consequences for noncompliance of all operational policies in accordance with organization policy and medical staff bylaws.
	Review perioperative performance metrics and progress toward annual targets, and take appropriate action when progress is not met or sustained over time.
	Create Surgeon Advisory Group (SAG) that will meet bi-monthly or at the discretion of the PEC. Charge this group with providing strategic and operational direction and advisory support to the PEC.
	Assemble and appoint working teams and task forces for deeper analysis and recommendations on performance improvement initiatives (i.e., scheduling and block utilization, throughput/optimization, etc.)
RELATIONSHIPS, RELIABILITY, EFFICIENCY, AND GROWTH	See Surgical Services Functional Chart
	See Department Dashboard

FIGURE 2.1   Sample PEC Charter (continued)

Surgeon Advisory Group
CHARTER

START DATE: TBD
SPONSOR(s): Perioperative Executive Committee (PEC)
CHAIR: Dr. Doctor
MEMBERS:

NAME	TITLE	AREA
Dr. Doctor	Surgical Services Medical Director	Anywhere Hospital
TBD		
TBD		
TBD		
TBD		
TBD		
TBD		
TBD		
TBD		
TBD		
TBD		

1. PURPOSE

This operational committee will consist of 8–12 surgeons across disciplines and will meet at regular intervals as a forum allowing surgeons to provide advice on recommended performance improvement and voice concerns regarding the management of perioperative resources and processes. In addition, they will provide a vital role in assisting the surgeon community in adapting to recommended performance improvement throughout the department. The scope of responsibilities will include the operations of perioperative services for the Main OR and the ASC. The Surgeon Advisory Group (SAG) will report its recommendations directly to the new Perioperative Executive Committee (PEC), which will have the power to evaluate and act on these recommendations.

2. STAKEHOLDERS

1. All patients in the operating room at Anywhere Hospital.
2. All direct care providers (RNs, CRNAs, MDs, PACs, Support Services) and department leadership.
3. Anywhere Hospital and Anesthesia leadership.

3. ANTICIPATED OUTCOMES

1. Provide assistance in procedural matters related to the operation of the operating room and pre-/postoperative areas.
2. Provide input into major operational decisions, including review of policies that impact the physician user of surgical services.
3. Review OR block utilization and other key effectiveness metrics (case start, case turnover).
4. Make recommendations to the PEC for changes in OR block allocations.
5. Participate in the service line strategic planning process.
6. Contribute to development and evaluation of a surgical services strategic plan that targets services and surgeons for growth consistent with the hospital's overall strategic plan and achieving the highest quality of care.
7. Review and evaluate quality of patient care provided during the perioperative period.

FIGURE 2.2   Sample SAG Charter

8. Monitor physician and patient satisfaction.
9. Provide input into operating and capital budgeting.
10. Review initiation of new technology/procedures.
11. Advise the PEC in all matters related to the ongoing efficiency and hospital's mission in the management of perioperative resources and processes.
12. Review performance metrics and offer suggestions to the PEC for improvements.
13. Assist in implementing new or revised programs, procedures, and policies.
14. Communicate with other medical staff members not available for meetings.
15. Provide consensus on the annual department operating plan with clear objectives, initiatives, and coordinated plans for the implementation of change.
16. Perform other responsibilities as requested by the PEC leadership.

4. AUTHORITY

1. The committee reports directly to the PEC and will review the achievement of goals and work accomplished annually.
2. The committee will use a consensus model for decision-making.

5. ROLE OF COMMITTEE MEMBERS

Each team member shall have an individual responsibility for examining and engaging in the process improvement efforts and contributing to the development of a culture that accepts and promotes change to enhance the patient experience of our department.

Key roles for the team are as follows:

Committee Chair:
The committee leader will keep members on track and help develop a system to guide the practice changes needed to enhance patient experience. This leader will evaluate members' participation and engagement and have the authority to add or remove individuals to benefit the patients and the committee. The leader will develop agenda items and work in collaboration with committee members to prioritize and evaluate initiatives beneficial to the patient and the department.

Committee Members:
Committee members will provide input and promote actions to support the cause of the committee. They will act out initiatives through their role to help promote change and cohesiveness among patients, families, and staff. Members will hold each other accountable for their actions and participation within the group. They are to help guide the practice to promote a culture of change and acceptance of best practices.

6. MEETING FREQUENCY, STRUCTURE, AND REPORTING MECHANISMS

1. The team will meet at least once a quarter or more at the request of the PEC and discretion of the members.
2. Meetings are targeted to run between 30 minutes and 1 hour.
3. Membership:
   - Medical Director of Surgical Services
   - Surgeon representatives from most surgical specialties
   - Ad hoc members (as identified based on meeting topics)
4. Additional regular invites:
   - Medical Directors, Anesthesia
   - VP, Clinical Operations
   - Director of Patient Care Surgical Services
   - Director of Patient Care Perioperative Services
5. Team members who are unable to attend will make every effort to notify the chair of the committee.
6. This committee reports to the PEC.

FIGURE 2.2   Sample SAG Charter (continued)

The Perioperative Governance Council (PGC)

The perioperative governance council (PGC) is similar to the PEC but is expanded to include a small number of surgeons who provide input on surgeon practice as a substitute for the surgeon advisory group. This type of structure works well for smaller organizations and reduces the burden of multiple meetings on physicians and other hospital leaders. The PGC connects with the larger department of surgery for the same purposes as the surgeon advisory group.

With the PEC or PGC management models, all performance-improvement or perioperative standing committees are realigned to report to the PEC/PGC. The PEC/PGC, in turn, typically reports directly to the organization's senior executive team and indirectly to the medical executive committee. The group needs to obtain and provide input from additional department leaders and physicians. This is accomplished by maintaining a surgeon advisory group (SAG) and a department leadership group.

The Department Leadership Group

The department leadership group (DLG) relates to the PEC in a similar manner to the SAG. The DLG typically includes:

- All key perioperative services department leaders with responsibility for managing nursing and support services (scheduling, OR, day surgery, PACU, sterile processing, etc.)

- Other key support leaders such as business managers, materials management, and information systems.

- The PEC provides direction to the DLG and, in turn, receives input and updates on key issues that need to be addressed.

CRITICAL ROLE OF ANESTHESIA SERVICES

The alignment of anesthesia services also is critical to the success of the governance structure. Anesthesia needs to be represented as active members of the PEC/PGC. The anesthesia chairperson, or designee, is typically a member of this group.

This role is filled by an anesthesiologist and dedicated to daily resource management. Time commitment may vary from 30% to 50% of a full-time equivalent (FTE) or more—especially during the first year—for organizations with multiple and complex perioperative management issues. Responsibilities include codirecting the perioperative services with the department director on the daily management of resources and the enforcement of policy, procedures, or guidelines. This individual serves in an active role, along with patient care managers, in resolving conflicts such as surgical case scheduling and staff assignments and ensuring maximum operational efficiencies. This role is negotiated as a separate role with the anesthesia group and compensated based on fair market value rates (see Figure 2.3).

Additionally, given the vital role anesthesia leadership plays in day-to-day operational management, it may be important to appoint an Anesthesia Perioperative Medical Director (AMD) in an administrative capacity as a partner with nursing for managing resources.

Anesthesiology Perioperative Medical Director Role Expectations

Position Specifications:

1. Is board-certified anesthesiologist.

2. Meets requirements for medical staff.

3. Demonstrates the ability to communicate effectively with patients, physicians, and other clinical and administrative personnel.

4. Displays the following attributes:

    ■ Is clinically astute in the delivery of anesthesia to surgical patients.

    ■ Is respected by physicians and personnel involved in perioperative services.

    ■ Possesses excellent interpersonal skills.

    ■ Is team-oriented.

    ■ Contributes to the improvement of processes/systems in the operating room.

Position Summary:

The anesthesiology perioperative medical director will provide leadership for the surgeon/anesthesiology/nursing team in the operating room and will guide the processes for all pre-, intra-, and postoperative aspects of care for patients served by the program.

The services provided by the anesthesiology perioperative medical director will be customer centered. Major customers will include patients and their families, surgeons, anesthesiologists, and the community at large.

In addition to clinical issues, the anesthesiology perioperative medical director's responsibilities will include quality assurance/quality improvement of all anesthesiology-related activities in the operating room and related areas, utilization review monitoring, and general oversight for the program. The anesthesiology perioperative medical director will also facilitate cohesive, amiable, and productive working relationships among all groups involved in perioperative services—surgeons, anesthesiologists and other physicians; nursing staff; and nursing management. The anesthesiology perioperative medical director will make policy recommendations to perioperative program administrators and will serve on the Perioperative Executive Committee (PEC) and other appropriate committees.

The anesthesiology perioperative medical director will be part of the PEC to ensure an effective operating room program. All individuals in this group will have specific responsibilities to ensure their part of the program works effectively and joint/team responsibilities to ensure all parts integrate effectively to achieve the goals of the administration and the medical staff.

FIGURE 2.3   Anesthesiology Perioperative Medical Director Role
Expectations SHC

Used with permission from Sullivan Healthcare Consulting

Primary Duties and Responsibilities:

1. Provides leadership for the operating room team in the daily management of the OR schedule and of patients in the pre-, intra-, and postoperative stages of surgery. Surgeon access and timely case starts are a first priority.

2. In collaboration with surgeons, anesthesiologists, and nursing staff and management, establishes protocols for managing patients in all stages of surgery to promote high-quality and cost-effective delivery of care.

3. Verifies that qualified anesthesiology personnel are available to cover the daily surgical schedule for all hours of the program's operations.

4. Participates in scheduling policy development and monitoring and ensures compliance with established practice.

5. Adheres to standards of care and service within guidelines of regulatory agencies.

6. Safeguards the fiscal integrity of the program and joint development of surgeon, anesthesiologist, nursing staff, and patient strategies for efficient throughput.

7. Participates in the development and enforcement of policies and procedures regarding anesthesiology personnel and the administration of anesthesia to patients in the program.

8. Monitors the quality of anesthesia care rendered throughout the program as established by the chair/chief of the department of anesthesiology. This is to include the postsurgical evaluation of additional preoperative patient testing ordered in the holding area and of cancellations of scheduled patients on the day of surgery.

FIGURE 2.3 Anesthesiology Perioperative Medical Director Role Expectations SHC (continued)

Used with permission from Sullivan Healthcare Consulting

BEST PRACTICES FOR STARTING A COMMITTEE

When establishing a PEC, SAG, or PGC, follow these best practices to ensure success:

- Develop a clear charter for the group that defines responsibility, accountability, authority reporting relationships, key functions, standing and ad hoc membership, frequency of meetings, and expectations of attendance. Typically attendance is expected at 80% of all meetings. Some telephone conferencing may be allowed (see Figures 2.1 and 2.2).

- Make decisions based on objective facts and having the capability to deliver on the decisions being made. Agenda items are planned and coded as decision-making items, discussion items, and review of analytical reports. Decision items are a priority. To efficiently facilitate the agenda, supporting attachments are provided to members at least 3 days before meetings to allow for review and feedback. Rarely are agenda topics introduced at a meeting without being on the agenda and without supporting information.

- Follow up on items introduced by PEC/PGC meetings. Minutes, including action items, responsibilities, and target dates for completion, should be distributed within 24 hours of the meeting. In addition, it is helpful to include a short recap of action items in email reminders to specific members before the next meeting.

- Provide the PEC/PGC/SAG members with mentoring to understand the shared governance model and their role and function in this newer structure. Brief one-on-ones with each member may be helpful to reflect on meetings and their participation.

- Identify clear surgical services strategies to ensure the alignment of decision-making with strategy. Many organizations have overall strategic plans, but they may not tie specifically to every surgical specialty growth and development plan. Poor "strategy-to-operations" planning can result in decisions that are not supportable by the organization. For example, if a surgical department develops its own plan, without ensuring that it aligns with the strategic plan of the organization, resources may not be available for them to achieve their goals/objectives.

- Implement an annual operational plan consisting of specific objectives tied directly to organization strategy. Identify specific performance-improvement initiatives to meet these objectives, along with key performance targets. In addition, the PEC/PGC should send frequent and periodic updates to the entire surgical community on progress in meeting objectives. These take the form of update newsletters or bulletins highlighting changes to processes.

- Take time to celebrate successes to maintain support and foster morale among clinicians and staff as changes are made.

TRANSITIONING TO A SHARED DECISION-MAKING MODEL

Transitioning to a shared decision-making governance model is not without obstacles and challenges. Below are some additional tips that are helpful during the transition to a shared governance model:

- Expect some level of resistance from one or more members of the C-suite. This typically occurs when senior leaders realize the level of authority being given to the PEC/PGC. C-suite commitment to the model is critical. The teams must be supported in their authority to make decisions to ensure their success. Offering C-suite leaders an opportunity to attend PEC meetings is often a good way to address resistance.

- Surgeons, who may have developed a pattern of going to the C-suite to get their personal agendas on OR resources met, may also represent a barrier during this transition. In this new model, all C-suite leaders should be encouraged to steer surgeons to the PEC. When they do, the tendency of surgeons to circumvent the group will diminish.

■ Department directors need to make adjustments to leading their departments as well. Directors need to recognize that they are now part of a decision-making body and that unilateral decisions on their part need to be avoided. Bringing requests and obstacles to the new PEC/PGC will ensure better success as the group assumes its shared governance role. Partnering with the anesthesia medical director is also a new responsibility that needs to be nurtured and developed by department directors. Ultimately, directors will feel better supported and more effective in this newer model.

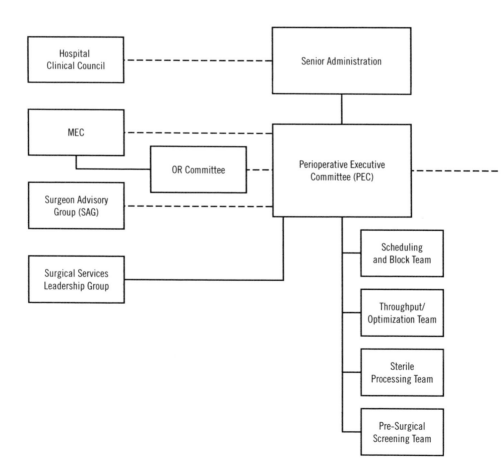

- Issues may arise with standing OR committees. In the shared governance model, one option for OR committees is to steer away from administrative management and refocus on clinical quality initiatives. In fact, this is an objective better suited for the medical staff. Both the PEC/PGC and the OR committee can concentrate on quality outcomes and measures. The OR committee can focus on best practice clinical pathways, and the PEC/PGC on ensuring alignment and management of resources to achieve the best quality outcomes. Another option is to eliminate the OR committee and have the function of oversight addressed in department of surgery meetings and the peer review process.

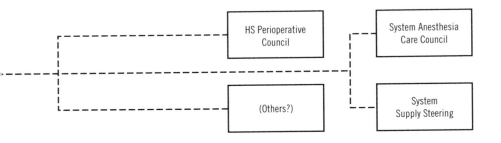

FIGURE 2.4   Anywhere Hospital Surgical Services Functional Chart

- Finally, it is important that the PEC/PGC communicate regularly with the overall hospital organizational structure and medical staff departments. Allocate time for members of the PEC/PGC to review their charter and address any questions or issues. Emphasis should be placed on the PEC/PGC serving clinical departments when resource management issues arise.

Establishing a well-functioning PEC/PGC is paramount to managing perioperative services effectively. The investment made in assessing the current organizational structure and, if needed, transitioning to a newer model of shared governance will pay back considerably in addressing any concerns and challenges in perioperative services.

Often it is helpful to develop a functional chart to identify the relationships of the newly formed PEC/SAG with that of other organization committees or councils. It may also contain committees that have been formed by the PEC. An example is provided in Figure 2.4.

EXECUTIVE LEADERSHIP LESSONS

- The complex healthcare environment requires an interdisciplinary and participative approach to management. Not only will all disciplines feel fully engaged in the process and outcomes, but a safe and error-free clinical environment can only be achieved when all care providers feel empowered to participate.

- Effective strategic leadership requires the alignment of the goals, objectives, and incentives for all clinicians and managers. While this is becoming increasingly difficult in an era of changing reimbursement models, it is nonetheless critical.

- Shared governance has repeatedly been demonstrated to enhance employee engagement, improve productivity, and empower staff to make decisions in the best interest of patient care at the point of service (as well as the interest of the organization).

- The governance structure for surgical services must be results-oriented with clearly defined roles and responsibilities, specifically of advisory roles.

REFERENCES

Blasco, T. (2013, November 7). Making the OR accountable. Hospital and Health Networks. https://www.hhnmag.com/articles/6092-making-the-or-accountable

Heiser, R. (2013). Using a best-practice perioperative governance structure to implement better block scheduling. *AORN 97*(1). http://dx.doi.org/10.1016/j.aorn.2012.10.007

OR Manager, Inc. (2007, January). Models for governance of the OR. *OR Manager,23*(1), 1–5. Retrieved from https://pdfs.semanticscholar.org/6714/f928c47ba2430c1c7ddeb80fce924651be58.pdf

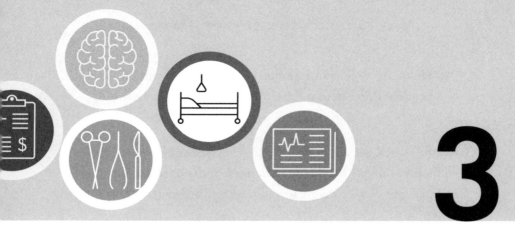

3

LEADERSHIP AND ORGANIZATION

Chapter 2 reviewed the need for a governance body focused on decision-making and resource management to ensure the effective delivery of care in operating rooms. Once an organization has established a multidisciplinary governance model for managing surgical services resources, numerous questions will arise:

- Is it the most meaningful structure for that particular organizational culture, and specifically for the culture of the medical staff?

- Will this structure effectively serve strategic and operational goals?

- Where should the department report within the broader organization as a means to ensure the strongest operational alignment?

- What should the organizational structure look like based on the size and scope of the department?

- Who should fill the key leadership roles? Are these roles effective?

- How can succession planning be hardwired to minimize dependency on external recruitment firms when leaders turn over?

Given the significant organizational impact, these governance bodies should report directly to the top leadership of the organization, most often the CEO or executive leadership team. The key questions then become:

- Where should the surgical services department report?

- What reporting structure will support a shared governance model and ensure surgeon and anesthesia commitment and utmost participation?

- What is the best means to ensure that surgical services is in complete alignment with the organization's strategic plan and is thereby providing a maximum financial contribution?

ORGANIZATIONAL ALIGNMENT OF SURGICAL SERVICES

In traditional organizational structures, the surgical services department has reported to nursing services because the majority of healthcare providers in the operating room are nurses and other clinical support staff. However, this structure has led to significant challenges, including lack of surgeon engagement and lack of shared leadership participation. There is a growing trend for the department to report to other operational leaders, such as the VP of operations or directly to the COO, recognizing that in many organizations a nurse executive holds these roles. There have even been instances of the department reporting to finance.

This debate over proper alignment highlights the complexity of the department. Therefore, a matrixed reporting relationship, though difficult, may be required. It is not unusual for the department director to have several superiors, necessitating effective communication channels and clearly defined roles and responsibilities. In addition to managing nursing care, the department director is required to work closely with the administrators over finance, materials management, the medical staff, and other non-nursing departments such as quality and risk management, radiology, and pathology.

It's logical for surgical services to report to nursing due to the numerous nursing practice policies, procedures, and shared governance requirements—and the fact that the surgical patient is cared for within a larger nursing continuum. Competitive forces and consumer needs are driving healthcare organizations to eliminate functional silos whereby patients are burdened with the need to navigate complex environments. Additionally, surgical services nursing care units need to be active in nursing and unit executive councils. All healthcare regulatory and accrediting organizations, including The Joint Commission, Det Norske Veritas Healthcare (DNV), the American Osteopathic Association, and the Centers for Medicare and Medicaid (CMS) require the chief nursing officer to provide oversight of the nursing care within these departments. Therefore, if alternative organizational alignment outside of nursing services is decided upon, a process and responsibilities for nursing oversight needs to be defined.

The benefits most often cited for having surgical services report to administration include:

- Direct connectivity and access for resolving day-to-day problems

- Developing organizationally integrated operational plans

- Implementation of performance-improvement objectives

Successful operational planning for surgical services requires close working relationships and mutual alignment of objectives with several of the non-nursing administrative departments. For example, cost management objectives will require the leaders from the medical staff, materials management, and the operating room to have common goals, execution strategies, and tactics. Sustainable gains in efficiency will require working closely with medical staff offices, registration, and admitting for the preadmission and preoperative workflows, among other things.

Another challenge is a trend among health systems to consolidate several departments that are integral to the surgical services department, such as scheduling, finance, and supply chain. Regardless of where the formal alignment occurs, at a minimum health system organizations should strive to establish a system-wide surgical services council consisting of surgical services leaders from each hospital as well as the consolidated departments to provide a forum to develop consistent objectives, strategies, and tactics.

OPTIONS FOR DESIGNING AN ORGANIZATIONAL MODEL

The size and scope of the surgical services department are the first considerations in developing an organizational model. Quite logically, the organizational model for a large department consisting of 30 or more operating rooms located in multiple sites will take on different dimensions than for single-site, midsize, or smaller departments.

Typically, larger organizations have a separate ambulatory surgery unit requiring integration within the larger department. In the case of multiple surgical locations and a large number of direct reports, multiple managers or coordinators will likely be necessary to provide adequate direction to personnel and the supervision of daily operations.

Key Roles

Determining the key roles required and the extent of responsibilities for each are also important considerations. Typically, a registered nurse manager-level position is established with responsibility for the key patient care units and functional areas. Larger operating room departments may require more than one manager, each assigned to multiple surgical specialties. For example, separate manager positions would be established for orthopedics-spine, general-urology-GYN, and ENT-plastics. In smaller departments, a single OR manager may be appropriate with coordinator-level positions over the surgical specialties. More considerations for surgical specialty management are reviewed in Chapter 6, "Nursing Management in Surgical Services."

Similarly, perianesthesia units in larger departments may need separate managers for preoperative and postoperative areas, while smaller departments would need only a single manager, with coordinators providing daily supervision of patient flow and nurse assignments.

Other key roles to consider are:

- Operating Room Control Desk or Board Coordinator

- Scheduling and Postoperative Data Entry

- Supply Coordinator

- Department Educator

- Sterile Processing Manager

A final consideration when designing the organizational chart is whether other similar procedure-based units, such as endoscopy services, should be within the scope of the surgical services department. These patient care units have similar leadership knowledge and skill requirements and often may share clinical and support functions such as anesthesia services, supply chain, and sterile processing. In an era of cost containment, this may be a desirable model, presuming a reasonable span of control.

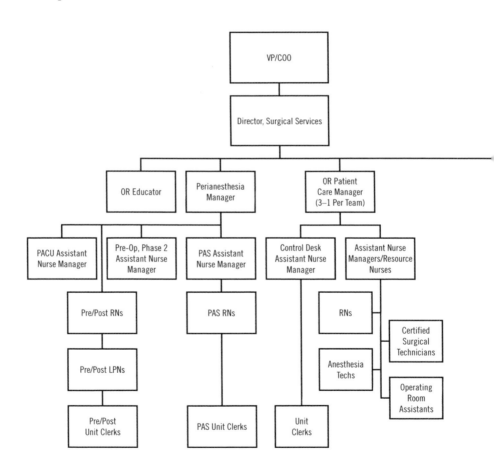

FIGURE 3.1 Single Director Organizational Chart

Single Director Model

The traditional organizational model for midsize or smaller departments is a single department director reporting to the CNO or a vice president (see Figure 3.1). This position is usually titled perioperative services director and encompasses all clinical units and functional areas within the department. Each of these units or areas has an assigned manager reporting to the director. These units and functional areas would include operating rooms, preadmission, preoperative and postoperative care units, and functional or clinical support areas such as scheduling, sterile processing, and supply.

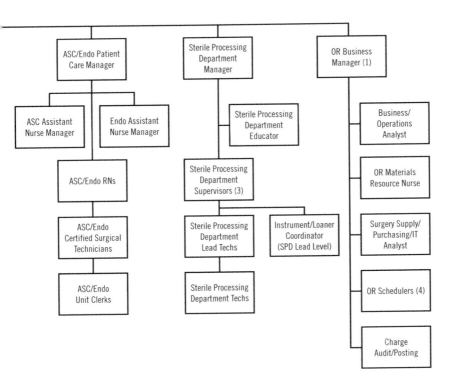

For the department director role, there are several considerations. The surgical services department is a complex and dynamic operation, necessitating that a director has a manageable span of control in order to be successful. A dual director model may be considered for large or complex departments, or when the number of direct reports exceeds 8 to 10.

Dual Director Models

There are two forms of dual director models. One splits the clinical units into administrative and support areas. The clinical director oversees all direct patient care units; a registered nurse typically fills this position. The administrative director would oversee the areas of scheduling, sterile processing, supply management, and other department business

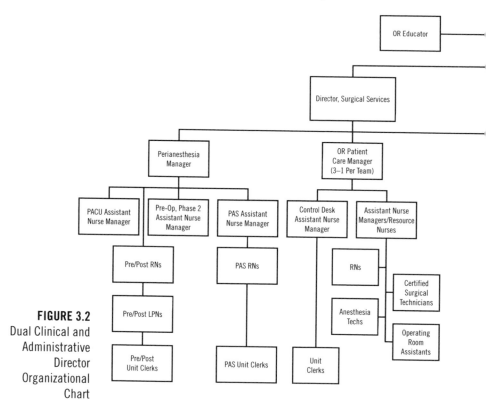

FIGURE 3.2
Dual Clinical and Administrative Director Organizational Chart

management functions such as budget management. This position requires a candidate with business management knowledge and skills; this individual would not need a clinical background.

The dual director model allows for increased focus over both clinical and administrative areas of responsibility. Ensuring these two directors work collaboratively and support each other is critical to their success. It is important to closely manage the risk for the two directors to disagree on issues related to the management of the department. It is also important to provide clear roles and responsibilities between the two directors to avoid confusion for physicians and hospital staff (see Figure 3.2).

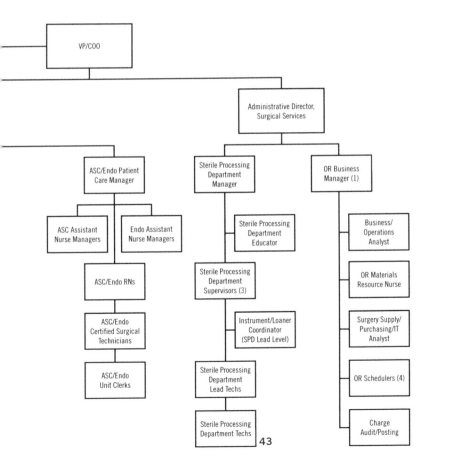

43

Another variant on the dual director model for large departments is to split the department between two clinical directors (who are typically registered nurses). One clinical director, titled the operating room or surgical services director, would have primary responsibly for the operating rooms, scheduling, and sterile processing. The second

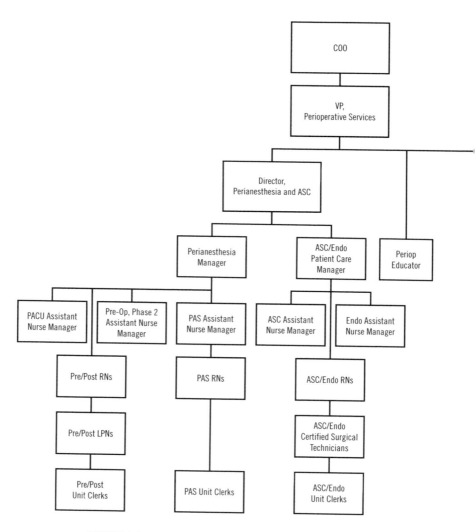

FIGURE 3.3   Clinical Dual Director Organization Chart

clinical director—titled the perianesthesia director—would have primary responsibility for the preadmission, preoperative, and post-operative units. This structure reflects the different clinical knowledge required for the operating room and perianesthesia patient care (see Figure 3.3).

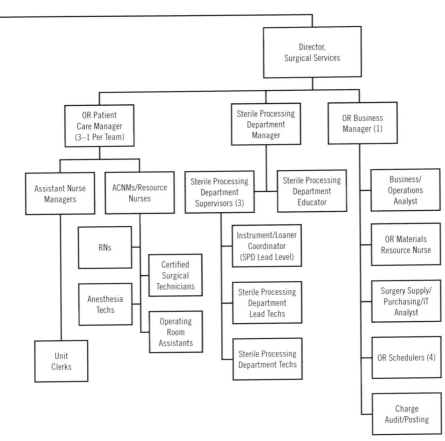

Vice President or Assistant Vice President Leadership

An emerging trend in large organizations is to assign a vice president (VP) or assistant vice president (AVP) over the surgical services department. This occurs most often when surgical services department leadership is given the direct responsibility for growing case volume. The rationale is to move the key business growth responsibilities closer to operational leaders who have solid relationships with the surgical departments and key surgeon leadership.

Legacy models and other organizational constraints may hamper the selection of an effective contemporary model, as well as the department leader titles. Human resources (HR) departments are typically charged with maintaining parity and equity throughout the organization and may require uniform titles and responsibilities. This same dynamic also may occur within a single hospital. Close working relationships need to be established with HR departments and HR leadership to understand the unique dynamics and needs of the surgical services environment. This will help determine the best organizational model and roles.

DEVELOPMENT AND SOURCING OF KEY LEADERS

Many healthcare executives are faced with the question of whether they have effective surgical services leaders. As noted, these departments drive a significant percentage of the hospital's revenue and are at the forefront of industry disruptive forces. Questions may stem from surgeons' complaints about unresponsive leaders; ongoing poor operational, financial, or quality measures; or high staff vacancy and turnover rates. While historically a department director may have achieved success in that role, the complexity of the value-driven model may require a closer look.

Healthcare executives should conduct a thorough and objective assessment of current surgical services leaders to identify their management knowledge, skills, and abilities. In some cases, a transition may be required; at a minimum, the review should result in a specific ongoing development plan for ineffective incumbents. An early assessment and action plan is critical for maintaining stability in this area.

One of the most arduous challenges for healthcare organizations is finding and developing surgical services leaders. National recruiters have expressed that sourcing candidates for a surgical services director role is very challenging and may take six months or more to fill vacant positions. Most of these recruiting websites consistently post 20 or more openings for their contracted clients. These vacancies have been created due to the extreme challenges of the role, the lack of progressive growth and development programs for surgical services leaders, and poor succession planning. Most recruiters are seeking to fill a surgical services leadership position due to an organization deciding the incumbent director is not a good fit for the department needs. When interviewing these candidates, pay careful attention not only to an individual's knowledge, skills, and experience, but to past professional experiences and organizational culture compatibility.

Growing Leaders Internally

Historically, the majority of department directors have had a nursing background and have advanced their careers as operating room staff nurses prior to working in progressive leadership or educational roles in the surgical services department. It is not uncommon to hear that these nurse were often initially identified as the best clinical nurse in the department. Their skills likely include problem-solving and decision-making in clinical care delivery. When moving into a leadership role, these basic skills need to be transferred to management problem-solving and decision-making processes. On-the-job development was often provided by senior hospital leaders and augmented through professional journals or conference attendance designed specifically for surgical services leaders.

This traditional sourcing model is not sustainable, though, because fewer nurses are interested in a management career track, and the emerging challenges of the role have far exceeded this informal track of management development. Additionally, the national nursing shortage is disproportionately impacting surgical services because it is a specialty underrepresented in baccalaureate educational programs; therefore, nurses are graduating with little exposure to the operating room in their clinical education. Fewer staff nurses entering the specialty suggest fewer in the leadership pipeline.

Leadership Development Programs

Today, healthcare organizations are providing management development programs focused on basic and advanced leadership training. In addition to these employer programs, there are leadership development programs in healthcare and other management industries focused on creating future leaders. These programs provide exposure to management principles required by leaders in a variety of industries and are designed to provide the basic strategies, methodologies, tactics, and tools that trainees could apply to their setting. Most are provided by professional organizations or through collegiate executive educational programs such as the Association of periOperative Registered Nurses (AORN), the Competency and Credentialing Institute (CCI), Harvard Business School, NYU Stern, and Northwestern Kellogg.

A DAY IN THE LIFE OF A SURGICAL SERVICES LEADER

Successful surgical services leaders report working a minimum of 10 hours a day. The leader needs to be present before the start of the surgical day to conduct rounds, engage with staff and physicians, and observe the flow of patient care. These actions will build strong relationships and provide early insight to any operational problems that need to be addressed.

The typical day for a surgical services leader consists of activities that affect operational efficiency, including staffing, scheduling, performance and quality improvement, financial management, and the growth of the business. These same successful leaders report they end their days either by attending hospital management meetings or by following up with clear communications to their direct reports and reviewing progress on operational objectives.

Despite the demanding schedule, healthcare executives must encourage surgical services leaders to schedule personal growth and development time.

Alternatives to the OR Nurse Surgical Services Leader

Over the course of the past 10 years, there has been an emergence of alternatives to the tradition of promoting operating room nurses to the surgical services director role. Anesthesiologists, surgeons, CRNAs, perianesthesia nurse leaders, non-OR experienced nurses, and healthcare administrators have been successfully placed in department leadership roles. Organizations faced with a department director transition or with a long-term vacancy should evaluate these alternatives and ask whether an experienced OR nurse is the best fit for the role. There is little doubt that a candidate with this experience brings a valuable and broad knowledge and understanding of patient care delivery and managing the variety of direct and indirect activities. The experience gained in "growing up in the OR" will provide insight into the multitude of dynamics in the surgical services arena. For smaller departments, the experience of staff nursing is invaluable when needing to step into the

OR suite for a short-term staffing crisis. Selecting a non-OR nurse will create some anxiety with the OR staff that requires careful management and communication.

Physicians may also be a viable option for filling this role. Physicians (surgeons or anesthesiologists) may have a better understanding of colleagues' needs and have a respected peer relationship within the physician community. They may be able to provide valuable insight into market trends and competitive forces.

Many physicians are now attending continuing education programs and MBA or MHA programs to enhance their understanding of the management process and prepare themselves for administrative roles. Successful physicians in the department leadership role also invest time in building strong relationships with nursing and other department support staff.

It is important to note the distinction between the physician in the department leadership role and that of a physician in a medical director role. Typically, the surgical services department will have a governance body that will include anesthesia and surgeon medical directors (see Chapter 2, "Governance and Managing Resources"). These roles are valuable for managing resources and decision-making on a day-to-day basis, but they do not hold the same responsibilities as that of the department director.

Certified registered nurse anesthetists (CRNAs) and perianesthesia nurse leaders are also a viable alternative for holding the director role given their extensive backgrounds in caring for surgical patients and, often, serving as members of the surgical services leadership team. Many CRNAs have served in a leadership capacity as chief CRNA and are experienced in the dynamics of the operating room environment.

Another source for surgical services leaders is experienced nurses without an OR background. Typically, these nurses have been managers or directors in critical care or obstetrics and have knowledge of the nursing process and management experience that transfers well into the operating room. Many times, these non-OR nurse leaders will attend the OR department orientation to gain basic knowledge and skills of the OR nurse.

A non-nurse administrative leader with experience in managing another hospital department could also fill the department director role, if this person has a solid management background and the ability to adapt to a unique clinical setting. This option should be considered when there is a strong team of nurse managers who can assist the administrative director in managing the clinical processes.

SUCCESSION PLANNING

Succession planning has been identified as critical to the success of any organization. Numerous articles have been published calling attention to a looming nurse shortage as the workforce ages without a commensurate inflow of students entering nursing programs (see Chapter 6, "Nursing Management in Surgical Services). This same dynamic is occurring in the surgical services area to an even greater extent because there are few college nursing programs providing operating room nursing content in their curricula (see Chapter 6). This shortage is reflected in an analysis of the state of OR managers. *OR Manager* has been conducting salary and OR workforce studies for 17 years. The most recent study, in 2017, reports the average age of an OR leader as 53.82 years, 5 years higher than in 2015 (48.8 years). When asked about retirement, 20% responded with plans to retire in 4 to 5 years, with another 20% planning to retire by 2026, for a combined 42% transition to retirement (Saver, 2017).

Development of Perioperative Leadership

Organizations need to identify potential surgical services leaders and provide opportunities and experiences for growth and development into management roles. The most successful organizations have conducted succession-planning programs in which each leader has identified, by name, two or three potential staff who could be groomed for management roles. These high performers typically desire a career plan, including additional management responsibilities and development experiences. Once identified, the organization will begin to make an investment in their growth and development, which often includes the opportunity to participate on unit councils, performance-improvement activities, and various other teams to gain insights and experience into managing surgical services—both the processes and the human resources. Concurrently, they also should receive basic management education to increase their knowledge and ability to manage others, effectively run a department, and build the business.

A similar process should be conducted for management-level leaders to identify their potential for development as department directors. They should be enrolled in management development programs sponsored by either the healthcare organization or external sources. While several great programs exist, there is at least one specific to surgical services management: Certified Surgical Services Manager, provided by the Competency & Credentialing Institute (CCI, 2018).

Common Barriers to Succession Planning

Existing barriers to succession planning require immediate attention. These barriers include:

- **Degree requirements.** A minimum of a BSN is typically required for the manager level, and often a master's degree for department director. Established by the Institute of Medicine (IOM, 2010) *Future of Nursing* report, these requirements are evidence based and a necessity in an industry that is becoming increasingly complex, with rapidly expanding technology. In fact, on December 18, 2017, the state of New York passed legislation requiring a baccalaureate or higher degree within 10 years of initial license (Gooch, 2017). An advanced degree is necessary for leadership roles and should be established as a mandatory requirement for promotion into a leadership position. The operating room historically has had fewer nurses with advanced degrees than other nursing areas, but this trend is rapidly changing. Most organizations are now requiring advanced degrees for these roles to meet higher expectations of the role and to meet requirements for recognition, such as Magnet status.

- **Transitioning from hourly pay to a salaried position.** An OR nurse's total salary is frequently higher than entry-level manager roles. This occurs because an OR nurse is usually required to work a designated number of on-call hours, frequently earning overtime, which can drive total salary to well above the fixed salary of a manager. Although it is true that there are inherent benefits in the career evolution to management, including no longer being required to work on-call, the average manager works approximately 50 hours a week. Setting competitive compensation is an important factor when enticing staff to make the transition to management.

- **Awareness of significant challenges associated with the role.** Staff nurses often observe firsthand the challenges inherent in surgical services management, making them reluctant to transition to a management path. Establishing leadership mentoring programs is one successful way to address these concerns and help candidates make the mental shift required for a management role (see Figure 3.4).

COMPARISON OF SURGICAL SERVICES ROLES AND RESPONSIBILITIES

OR MEDICAL DIRECTOR	NURSING SCHEDULE COORDINATOR
■ Manages the daily schedule. ■ Takes the lead and is final arbiter on placement of cases and determining which case should be booked into the evening. ■ Oversees and approves the long-term operating room schedule. ■ Reviews the anticipated schedule for the next day and makes adjustments to maximize utilization. ■ Provides input to the department director and manager on operational and capital budget planning. ■ Enforces scheduling policy and makes recommendations for improvements to the OR governance committee. ■ Assists the OR governance committee with strategic and operational planning.	■ Coordinates all resources in the delivery of patient care in the operating room. ■ Collaborates with the OR medical director on decisions regarding placement of cases in the operating rooms. ■ Coordinates with pre- / post-op care units, OR staff, and sterile processing on planning and delivery of patient care. ■ Communicates the OR schedule and any changes made with surgeons, anesthesia, surgical services staff, and other hospital departments. ■ Supervises the control desk staff. ■ Makes out nursing assignments, including lunch and break relief.
SURGICAL SERVICES DIRECTOR	OR MANAGER
■ Represents the department at hospital department director meetings. ■ Overall surgical services department operation and budget planning. ■ Works with department managers and coordinators to plan and supervise patient care delivery and support services for the department. ■ Responsible for evaluation, growth, and development of managers and coordinators.	■ Plans and supervises patient care delivery in the operating room. ■ Coordinates OR staff schedules with Nursing Schedule Coordinator. ■ Coordinates the need for support from biomedical engineering, engineering, environmental services, and other hospital departments. ■ Responsible for evaluation, growth, and development of operating room staff. ■ Responsible for planning and managing the operating room budget.
ANESTHESIA COORDINATOR	
■ Makes out anesthesia assignments, including lunch and break relief. ■ Maintains efficiency of the daily management of anesthesia services. ■ Identifies anesthesia equipment needs to the department director and manager.	

FIGURE 3.4 Surgical Services Management: Comparison of Roles and Responsibilities

EXECUTIVE LEADERSHIP LESSONS

- When assessing the leadership structure of the surgical services department, begin with operational alignment. Often, new executives look to the incumbent leaders as the source of dysfunction within the operation, rather than assessing the department's alignment with the overall strategy of the organization. For instance, if the strategic plan calls for significant volume and revenue growth, does the leadership structure provide the resources and sufficient time to assess market trends and the competitive landscape, meet with surgeons, construct business plans, and evaluate the current revenue streams? Often the organizational structure is focused on daily operations. Although critically important, this structure will not necessary fuel new revenue growth.

- There is no best reporting relationship for surgical services. Whether surgical services reports through the nursing department or the CEO or COO is often decided by the size of the organization, the maturity of the shared governance leadership model, the strategic imperatives including aggressive growth plans, and the overall alignment with the medical staff. As larger integrated systems evolve, strategic alignment as a system based on a product line model is an effective means to minimize duplication of services, prevent internal competition for patients and surgeons, and negotiate with payers.

- No matter the direct reporting structure, the environmental complex suggests that leaders need to be comfortable with matrixed relationships, including accountability to the executive team, medical staff leadership, finance, and various clinical departments.

- To effectively lead a surgical services department, a manager must be able to convey the mission, vision, and values of the organization; effectively manage the fast-paced daily operations; create an environment that is safe for patients and staff, including surgeons; verify compliance with a myriad of regulatory requirements; and evaluate and develop personnel. This is in addition to monitoring and growing the business—a tall order indeed.

- Operating rooms across the country are facing a looming shortage of qualified clinical staff, particularly nurses. In some areas, executives are forced to temporarily shut down operating rooms due to insufficient staffing. In an effort to prevent this calamity, hospitals can develop their own training programs and formal succession planning processes.

REFERENCES

Competency & Credentialing Institute (CCI). (2018). *CCSM—Certified Surgical Services Manager*. Retrieved from http://cc-institute.org/cssm

Gooch, K. (2017, December 20). New York State passes 'BSN in 10' nursing education legislation. *Becker's Hospital Review*. Retrieved from https://www.beckershospitalreview.com/human-capital-and-risk/new-york-state-passes-bsn-in-10-nursing-education-legislation.html

Institute of Medicine (IOM). (2010). *The future of nursing: Leading change, advancing health*. Washington, DC: The National Academic Press.

Saver, C. (2017, September 20). OR leaders report strong job satisfaction but weak compensation. *OR Manager, 33*(10). Retrieved from https://www.ormanager.com/leaders-report-strong-job-satisfaction-weak-compensation/

4

BUDGET AND FINANCIAL MANAGEMENT

Perioperative services is one of the largest revenue- and expense-producing departments within an organization (Weiss, Elixhauser, & Andrews, 2014). A recent California study reported the mean (SD) cost for one minute of OR time in hospitals was $37.45 (Childers & Maggard-Gibbons, 2018). That is a cost of nearly $2250.00 per hour! Optimizing the financial performance of perioperative services is, therefore, crucial to the organization. In addition, changes in healthcare payment models are evolving from volume-based to value-based reimbursement models, shifting the focus to the impact of quality outcomes on reimbursement. These are just a few of the multiple challenges healthcare leaders face in managing surgical services to attain the highest contribution margins.

The greatest opportunities to improve performance in perioperative services are in the active management of labor, supply, and surgical implant expenses.

Several cost-management initiatives and best practices have been deployed in the industry to reduce these expenses, but most have failed to achieve, or sustain, targeted savings levels.

Labor expenses are often driven by decisions made related to opening more operating rooms (ORs) than needed based on perceived demand and poor utilization, or in promises made to surgeons during recruitment or in existing program expansion.

Supply and surgical implant expenses can rise when surgeon requests to use new products are not reviewed without taking into account the potential impact on overall and ongoing department expense. Surgical implant expenses are for items such as mechanical devices (e.g., orthopedic total joints), general surgery mesh implants for hernia repair, or cardiac defibrillator devices. There are several manufacturers to choose from. Surgeons have traditionally chosen manufacturers based on the devices they were trained on or on companies surgeons may be working with in further development of an implant. In most cases, the healthcare organization will receive an implant request from the surgeon and is expected to make the purchase as requested. This leads to minimal opportunity to negotiate lower costs.

The surgical services leader can achieve the highest level of contribution margin when provided with sufficient resources (and time) to understand revenue and expense streams.

This chapter will start with background information to help readers understand the surgical services operational budgeting process and will then explore:

- Case volumes and the revenues they produce
- The process for establishing both labor and nonlabor costs

- Best practices to manage the drivers of these expenses

- Observations on managing the capital budget

THE SURGICAL SERVICES BUDGETING PROCESS

Typically, surgical services contain several cost centers for each unit, such as the operating room, preoperative, postoperative, and support areas (most notably, sterile processing). This chapter will focus primarily on the OR because it is most complex and is a driver of expenses for other patient care and support units.

Hospitals frequently use an adjusted historical approach to setting revenues and expenses in the OR. This involves establishing future budget levels by evaluating past budget levels and performance and using a correlation calculation that reflects volume increases or decreases. The most common budgeting method is based on case volume for each surgical specialty area or program, taking into consideration the differences in case types and the complexity of resources consumed by different specialties. For example, the cost of supplies and implants for an orthopedic total joint case will be much higher than supplies and implants used for a hernia repair.

Basing a budget on case volumes alone may not allow for calculation of some expenses that are actually driven by case *minutes,* with longer cases consuming more resources per case. A 4-hour case will obviously represent higher labor costs than a 1-hour case. It's important to include projections of total case minutes and case volumes when projecting expenses.

Using historical adjustments alone, however, may mean that some projections become invalid as time goes by. For example, adjusting staffing based on volume alone may not reflect the costs of adding staff to provide additional surgical assistance that fewer surgeons are providing.

In addition, process improvements that lead to increased throughput, or decreased costs of late starts or turnover, would impact the number of staff hours required. Therefore, some degree of zero-based budgeting (starting the budgeting process "from scratch" without reliance on past budget levels) on a periodic basis can help to confirm current demand and reset projections. This approach also can help raise confidence in the budget.

Understanding Case Volume

The projected case volume for each surgical specialty drives both budgeted revenue and expenses. Projected volumes should be established based on adjusting historical volume levels for key drivers of volume. Some of the more important considerations are:

- Realization of strategic objectives

- New clinical programs and growth or decline in current programs

- Changes to primary care physician practices and referral patterns

- Projected surgeon recruitment or loss

- Volume shifts from inpatient to outpatient

During what is generally an annual budgeting process, the finance department typically provides targeted case volumes based on the overall organization's strategic and operational plans, which are largely geared toward inpatient volumes. Only recently have hospital volume projections accounted for the shift from inpatient to outpatient surgery. The organization's strategic development and service line leaders produce the inpatient and outpatient projections that finance uses to produce the first round projected budget.

Typically, surgical case volume is distributed over the twelve months based on the total operative days in a month. It is important to note that case volume will probably fluctuate beyond this monthly allocation based on seasonality and other factors that are difficult to predict. These include vacation time for high-volume surgeons; absences related to annual association conferences; and a more recent trend of November-to-December surges in case volume due to patients' tendency to opt for elective surgery when they have already met their insurance deductibles.

Surgical service department leadership is then asked to review and confirm these projections or make any recommended changes. In doing this, perioperative services should seek and include input from leaders of both surgery and anesthesia, who may have more knowledge of impending surgical practice changes and the turnover or recruitment of new surgeons. The surgical services department leadership and governing body (see Chapter 2) should then forward the recommended budgeted case volumes back to the finance department.

It is important to note that any recommended changes to case volume, especially inpatient volume, will need to align with projected hospital admission projections. The surgical services department recommendations are reviewed by finance; often, any recommended case volume changes will need to be rigorously reviewed and then reconciled with other department budgets. Projected case volumes are finalized during a final budget review and before the overall hospital budget is closed. Any significant changes at this point should be reviewed with the surgical services department leadership and then used in planning the revenue and expense budget.

Understanding Revenue

Revenue is driven by the type and number of surgical cases being performed and the contractual agreements that have been established for
reimbursement. Contractual agreements vary with every organization
and are dependent upon individual payor negotiations. We recommend you review these with your finance department to gain insight
into how your organization is reimbursed for surgical procedures. All
reimbursement is driven by the charges captured in surgery. The typical
perioperative services budget contains gross revenue based on charges
for projected case volumes by surgical specialty. These gross charges are
not adjusted for contractual agreements; they are designed to serve as a
guide based on accurate charge-capture activities rather than actual net
revenue.

The charges applied are based on the *charge master*—or *charge descrip-
tion master* (CDM)—which is a list of all of the things that might be
billed to a patient. Each healthcare organization has its own charge
master, which includes a set of time-based and individual charges for
supplies and the use of some equipment. Time-based charges are given
in ranges of minute increments based on the complexity of cases or
surgical specialties. These charges are designed to recover the direct department expenses of labor, facility, depreciation, department overhead,
and other hospital allocations. These hospital allocations typically are
a portion of the expense for non-revenue producing hospital departments.

Individual supply or equipment charges are established, as these items
are initially purchased by the organization. Charges include a reasonable mark-up, which is applied to the acquisition cost. The total of the
acquisition and mark-up reflect the actual charge that will be included
in the charge master. Charges are adjusted annually based on projected
cost increases. The OR will probably be using some supply or implant

items that are not included in the charge master. When this occurs, the charge must be calculated and entered into the patient billing system. A surgical services department will have a charge reconciliation process that reviews all charges for a case and captures the need for adding a manual charge.

Some organizations have moved to establishing fixed charges for some procedures, either when contracting with payers or when the patient is the payer. These fixed charges work well for procedures and have demonstrated a consistent use of labor and supply expense. Fixed charges will also be included in the charge master.

It is common for surgical services department leaders to not fully understand what time-based charges include, because this is not a subject area covered in basic OR management courses. More than likely, the charges were established many years past and have not been reviewed by current leadership. Charge master reviews are not a high priority when compared with other needs for cost management. However, the charge master should be reviewed by the finance and surgical services departments and updated periodically to ensure accurate charges. Several organizations are now doing this annually.

Surgical services departments need to closely monitor the accuracy of charge capture in the charge reconciliation process. It is not infrequent for busy OR staff to miss entering a supply charge or inaccurately document an implant charge. This most often occurs when an item is not listed in the charge master. Whenever possible, all items that do not have a master charge code should be added to the charge master. Clear responsibilities should be identified by the surgical services leadership team for the review of charges, the identification of any questionable or missing charges, and reconciliation to the charge master. The department director should work with finance to ensure an efficient process is defined for managing charges and adding to the charge master.

LABOR EXPENSES

Healthcare organizations are service organizations with clinical care and administrative services being provided by people. Consequently, labor expense represents a significant portion of the overall healthcare organization's budget as well as the budget for surgical services.

Both direct and indirect labor expenses impact departments. Direct labor expenses include the cost of wages as well as payroll taxes, benefits, and workers' compensation insurance. Indirect labor expenses, often considered overhead, are expenses for staff who do not directly deliver the service.

All nursing patient care units will have both direct and indirect labor expenses; these expenses apply to surgical services. Our focus will be on the special considerations of the surgical services environment.

Labor expenses are driven by a plan of operations that is developed when a unit is opened to provide patient care. This plan of operations is often referred to as the *room coverage plan* or *resource hours*. Resource hours are established based on projected case volume and the strategic and operational goals of the hospital. For example, if the organization has plans to grow case volume, it may open more rooms and add more hours per room to accommodate growth. These rooms need to be staffed and ready to go as surgery scheduling accepts reservation requests from surgeons and their offices. More detail on surgery scheduling guidelines and setting levels of utilization are covered in Chapter 5, "Performance Management."

Because most surgical cases are elective, most surgical departments are not open and staffed at a constant level on a 24/7/365 basis. For instance, there may be a skeleton staff in the OR during late evenings and on weekends. Often OR and recovery room staff are on call, as needed, for any emergency procedures. The preadmission and day-of-surgery preoperative units usually only work the day shift and portions of the evening shifts.

Operating Room Clinical Labor

OR labor is made up primarily of staff that provide scrub and circulating duties in each OR suite. Scrub staff include surgical technicians (STs) or registered nurses (RNs). These staff members wear sterile garb and assist the surgical team by preparing and passing to the rest of the surgical team the needed instrumentation, supplies, implants, and some of the intraoperative medications for a surgical case. The circulator is an RN with responsibilities to ensure the surgical team has all the necessary supplies, instrumentation, and equipment available for the case, while also assessing patient need and monitoring the sterile field. The circulator also manages specimens and completes documentation of the case. Most cases require a scrub and circulator; some require a second scrub or circulator based on the complexity of the case (Association of periOperative Registered Nurses [AORN], 2018).

As covered earlier, OR labor expense and productivity will be directly affected by the number of resource hours that are set for each operating room and the targeted utilization rates. In addition, OR clinical staffing is directly affected by the number of rooms in operation and the number of staff assigned to each room. See Figure 4.1 for a typical OR staffing model.

	Day Of Week	Rooms Open	Hours Open	Hours Closed	Minimum Staff/ Room	Hours Open/ Room	Hours Open/ Day	Number Staff/ Shift	Staff Hours/ Day
ASU	Monday	3	7:00 AM	3:00 PM	2	8.0	24	6	48
	Tuesday	3	7:00 AM	3:00 PM	2	8.0	24	6	48
	Wednesday	3	7:00 AM	3:00 PM	2	8.0	24	6	48
	Thursday	3	7:00 AM	3:00 PM	2	8.0	24	6	48
	Friday	3	7:00 AM	3:00 PM	2	8.0	24	6	48
Main OR	Monday	6	7:00 AM	3:00 PM	2	8.0	48	12	96
	Tuesday	6	7:00 AM	3:00 PM	2	8.0	48	12	96
	Wednesday	7	7:00 AM	3:00 PM	2	8.0	56	14	112
	Thursday	7	7:00 AM	3:00 PM	2	8.0	56	14	112
	Friday	6	7:00 AM	3:00 PM	2	8.0	48	12	96
	Monday	4	3:00 PM	5:00 PM	2	2.0	8	8	16
	Tuesday	4	3:00 PM	5:00 PM	2	2.0	8	8	16
	Wednesday	4	3:00 PM	5:00 PM	2	2.0	8	8	16
	Thursday	4	3:00 PM	5:00 PM	2	2.0	8	8	16
	Friday	4	3:00 PM	5:00 PM	2	2.0	8	8	16
	Monday	2	5:00 PM	7:00 PM	2	2.0	4	4	8
	Tuesday	2	5:00 PM	7:00 PM	2	2.0	4	4	8
	Wednesday	2	5:00 PM	7:00 PM	2	2.0	4	4	8
	Thursday	2	5:00 PM	7:00 PM	2	2.0	4	4	8
	Friday	2	5:00 PM	7:00 PM	2	2.0	4	4	8
	Monday	1	7:00 PM	11:00 PM	2	4.0	4	2	8
	Tuesday	1	7:00 PM	11:00 PM	2	4.0	4	2	8
	Wednesday	1	7:00 PM	11:00 PM	2	4.0	4	2	8
	Thursday	1	7:00 PM	11:00 PM	2	4.0	4	2	8
	Friday	1	7:00 PM	11:00 PM	2	4.0	4	2	8
	Monday	1	11:00 PM	11:59 PM	2	1.0	0.9833	2	1.9667
	Tuesday	1	11:00 PM	11:59 PM	2	1.0	0.9833	2	1.9667
	Wednesday	1	11:00 PM	11:59 PM	2	1.0	0.9833	2	1.9667
	Thursday	1	11:00 PM	11:59 PM	2	1.0	0.9833	2	1.9667
	Friday	1	11:00 PM	11:59 PM	2	1.0	0.9833	2	1.9667
	Monday	1	12:00 AM	7:00 AM	2	7.0	7	2	14
	Tuesday	1	12:00 AM	7:00 AM	2	7.0	7	2	14
	Wednesday	1	12:00 AM	7:00 AM	2	7.0	7	2	14
	Thursday	1	12:00 AM	7:00 AM	2	7.0	7	2	14
	Friday	1	12:00 AM	7:00 AM	2	7.0	7	2	14
Saturday and Sunday		1	24 hour		2	24.0	24	2	48
	Saturday	1	7:00 AM	3:00 PM	2	8.0	8	2	16

		Day Of Week	Hours Open/ Day	Staff Ratio	Open Staffing Hours	Lunch Break	Float Staff	Fixed Hours	Benefit Time
ASU	7-3	Monday	24.0	2.0	48.0	4.5	8.0	60.5	9.1
		Tuesday	24.0	2.0	48.0	4.5	8.0	60.5	9.1
		Wednesday	24.0	2.0	48.0	4.5	8.0	60.5	9.1
		Thursday	24.0	2.0	48.0	4.5	8.0	60.5	9.1
		Friday	24.0	2.0	48.0	4.5	8.0	60.5	9.1
Main OR	7-3	Monday	48.0	2.0	96.0	9.0	16.0	121.0	18.2
		Tuesday	48.0	2.0	96.0	9.0	16.0	121.0	18.2
		Wednesday	56.0	2.0	112.0	10.5	16.0	138.5	20.8
		Thursday	56.0	2.0	112.0	10.5	16.0	138.5	20.8
		Friday	48.0	2.0	96.0	9.0	16.0	121.0	18.2
	3-5	Monday	8.0	2.0	16.0	0.0	2.7	18.7	2.8
		Tuesday	8.0	2.0	16.0	0.0	2.7	18.7	2.8
		Wednesday	8.0	2.0	16.0	0.0	2.7	18.7	2.8
		Thursday	8.0	2.0	16.0	0.0	2.7	18.7	2.8
		Friday	8.0	2.0	16.0	0.0	2.7	18.7	2.8
	5-7	Monday	4.0	2.0	8.0	0.0	1.3	9.3	1.4
		Tuesday	4.0	2.0	8.0	0.0	1.3	9.3	1.4
		Wednesday	4.0	2.0	8.0	0.0	1.3	9.3	1.4
		Thursday	4.0	2.0	8.0	0.0	1.3	9.3	1.4
		Friday	4.0	2.0	8.0	0.0	1.3	9.3	1.4
	7-11	Monday	4.0	2.0	8.0	0.0	1.3	9.3	1.4
		Tuesday	4.0	2.0	8.0	0.0	1.3	9.3	1.4
		Wednesday	4.0	2.0	8.0	0.0	1.3	9.3	1.4
		Thursday	4.0	2.0	8.0	0.0	1.3	9.3	1.4
		Friday	4.0	2.0	8.0	0.0	1.3	9.3	1.4
	11-Midnight	Monday	1.0	2.0	2.0	0.0	0.0	2.0	0.3
		Tuesday	1.0	2.0	2.0	0.0	0.0	2.0	0.3
		Wednesday	1.0	2.0	2.0	0.0	0.0	2.0	0.3
		Thursday	1.0	2.0	2.0	0.0	0.0	2.0	0.3
		Friday	1.0	2.0	2.0	0.0	0.0	2.0	0.3
	Midnight-7a	Monday	7.0	2.0	14.0	0.0	0.0	14.0	2.1
		Tuesday	7.0	2.0	14.0	0.0	0.0	14.0	2.1
		Wednesday	7.0	2.0	14.0	0.0	0.0	14.0	2.1
		Thursday	7.0	2.0	14.0	0.0	0.0	14.0	2.1
		Friday	7.0	2.0	14.0	0.0	0.0	14.0	2.1
	24 Hr	Saturday and Sunday	24.0	2.0	48.0	4.5	8.0	60.5	9.1
	7-3	Saturday	8.0	2.0	16.0	1.5	2.7	20.2	3.0
		Subtotals:	527.9		1055.8	76.5	157.3	1289.7	193.5

		FTEs
Open Staffing Hours:	1055.8	26.4
Lunch Break:	76.5	1.9
Float Staff:	157.3	3.9
Benefit Time:	193.5	4.8
Weekly Staffing Hours:	1483.1	37.1

FIGURE 4.1 OR Staffing Model

Some surgical cases will require a surgical assistant. This role may be filled by a physician (e.g., another surgeon, fellow, or resident) or by a nonphysician (e.g., a physician assistant, nurse practitioner, clinical nurse specialist, certified registered nurse, or surgical technician assistants). Providing surgical assistance has become a significant challenge for most organizations because reductions in surgeon reimbursement for surgical assisting has been significantly reduced or eliminated. It often is not cost effective for surgeons to employ a surgical assistant. Reimbursement for nonphysician surgical assistants in these roles has begun to improve to meet this need.

Typically, the medical staff bylaws address which surgical cases require assistance. In addition, the American College of Surgeons has recommended lists of procedures by surgical specialty (ACS, 2018). The Centers for Medicare and Medicaid Services (CMS) have specific guidelines for surgical assistance, which are used to govern need and reimbursement.

CMS and other payers have designated the surgical cases, conditions, and types of personnel that will be reimbursed (CMS, 2018). In some practices, the surgeon employs the surgical assistant; in others the hospital provides this service.

Maintaining an adequate supply of nonphysician providers is challenging. Cost-benefit analyses need to be conducted based on the level of demand to determine whether hospital employment or contracting for these services is most appropriate.

The remainder of OR labor consists of the department leadership team (see Chapter 3) and clinical support roles that provide assistance with supply distribution, transport, or environmental services. These support roles address nonclinical duties, keeping the overall costs of clinical labor minimized and allowing clinical staff to stay engaged in patient care. Some of this support may be provided by the hospital departments. During the budgeting process, it is important to evaluate these roles and determine necessary staffing numbers.

Perianesthesia Labor

Perianesthesia patient-care units are typically used during preadmission, the day of surgery preoperative, in the recovery room, and during phase two recovery for outpatients. These units are typically staffed with RNs and a patient care assistant role. Staffing for these units is typically determined based on safe nurse-to-patient care ratios. The American Society of PeriAnesthesia Nurses (ASPAN) recommends some of these ratios (ASPAN, 2017). For example, staffing in the recovery room is typically an average of one RN to two patients. The preoperative and phase two recovery units are often merged and staffed at a one RN–to–three patient ratio. Nursing care demands for preoperative units are growing as more outpatient surgery is transitioned to ambulatory surgery centers and more acute and complex patients remain in the hospital setting. See Figure 4.2 for a typical perianesthesia staff model.

Hour of Day	Total Number Patients	Average Number Patients	Minimum Number Patients
0:00-1:00	95	4.32	0
1:00-2:00	94	4.27	0
2:00-3:00	91	4.14	0
3:00-4:00	83	3.77	0
4:00-5:00	80	3.64	0
5:00-6:00	79	3.59	0
6:00-7:00	78	3.55	0
7:00-8:00	80	3.64	0
8:00-9:00	101	4.59	0
9:00-10:00	189	8.59	3
10:00-11:00	273	12.41	5
11:00-12:00	336	15.27	5
12:00-13:00	391	17.77	13
13:00-14:00	451	20.50	14
14:00-15:00	486	22.09	16
15:00-16:00	495	22.50	15
16:00-17:00	495	22.50	16
17:00-18:00	445	20.23	10
18:00-19:00	399	18.14	11
19:00-20:00	358	16.27	10
20:00-21:00	327	14.86	8
21:00-22:00	315	14.32	7
22:00-23:00	211	9.59	3
23:00-24:00	186	8.45	0
Note: Data represents one full month (6/98)			
Staff ratio calculated using average + one standard deviation			
ASPAN guideline: minimum PACU staffing of 2			
Staff hours=7.5 hrs per day			

Maximum Number Patients	Standard Deviation	Average + 1 Standard Deviation	Staff Ratio (1:2)	Staff Ratio (4:6)
8	2.85	7.17	3.58	4.78
9	2.91	7.19	3.59	4.79
8	2.95	7.09	3.54	4.72
8	2.76	6.53	3.27	4.35
8	2.63	6.26	3.13	4.18
8	2.59	6.19	3.09	4.12
8	2.58	6.12	3.06	4.08
8	2.50	6.13	3.07	4.09
10	2.86	7.45	3.72	4.96
15	3.61	12.20	6.10	8.13
20	4.35	16.76	8.38	11.17
24	4.68	19.95	9.98	13.30
27	3.70	21.48	10.74	14.32
28	4.13	24.63	12.31	16.42
31	3.82	25.91	12.95	17.27
32	4.26	26.76	13.38	17.84
29	3.41	25.91	12.95	17.27
30	5.22	25.45	12.72	16.96
27	3.98	22.12	11.06	14.74
24	3.95	20.23	10.11	13.48
22	3.86	18.72	9.36	12.48
37	6.00	20.31	10.16	13.54
17	4.06	13.65	6.82	9.10
16	4.38	12.84	6.42	8.56
	Staff Hours:		184	245
	Min. # Staff Per Day:		24.47	32.62
	Benefit Time (22%):		5.38	7.18
	Total FTEs Recommended:		**29.85**	**39.80**

FIGURE 4.2   Alt Sample Perianesthesia Staff in Model

Clinical Support Labor

Clinical support is the final area of surgical services staffing and typically requires several types of clinical support staff. These roles include:

- Department managers and supervisors
- Specialty team leaders (see Chapter 6, "Nursing Management in Surgical Services")
- Patient care technicians for transport
- Environmental services (ES) staff, which may be part of the hospital's ES department
- Sterile processing

NONLABOR EXPENSES

Nonlabor expenses in perioperative services consist of supplies, surgical implants, instrumentation, and equipment and contract services. These types of expenses have grown significantly due to the increasing use of technology in surgical cases. Gaining an understanding of these expenses is critical to developing tactics to manage them cost-effectively while achieving high-quality care outcomes.

Supplies and Implants

Historically, the expense lines for supplies and implants were combined under a single category of medical-surgical supplies. Experience has shown this single expense line typically accounted for up of 80% of all nonlabor expenses and was difficult to manage because surgical services leadership needed to sort through large ledgers of data to identify groups of high-cost items. Over the last decade, most organizations have broken this category down into individual expense lines for at least implants and sutures. Some have further sorted the expenses by individual surgical specialties, like orthopedics and cardiac. This has allowed for a better understanding of the use and costs of these types of supplies and for tracking and trending specific categories of costs. Even with this separation and sorting, the medical-surgical supply line for a department continues to contain multiple types of supplies and remains the largest supply cost category.

Success in managing supply and implant costs lies in the ability to link these expenses to the volume and types of cases being performed. For example, as monthly orthopedic total joint cases increase, a rise in orthopedic supplies and implants would be expected. Generally, this is true; however, depending on how expenses are captured and reported by finance, some of these costs could be reported in a different month than the surgery occurred. For example, an orthopedic implant may be used in May but not be reported on the ledger until June. If you have a higher-than-expected number of total joints in one month, and then compare that for expenses on that same month, you will arrive at a lower average orthopedic implant cost per procedures. The following month this average might skyrocket when orthopedic implant expenses are compared to normal case volume.

In addition, there may be errors in capturing and recording expense items to the appropriate line-item expense. For example, a hiatal hernia implant mesh may not be reported under general surgery implants, but buried in the general medical-surgical expense line. Great care needs to be exercised to review the detailed ledgers of cost reporting to ensure costs are assigned correctly before any reliable analysis can be conducted.

Contract Services

Expenses for contract services typically represent clinical and clinical support activities that have been determined to be more cost effective through external sources (e.g., surgical assistance, intraoperative neurological monitoring, perfusion, equipment maintenance, and biomedical service). These service contracts warrant periodic review to ensure performance metrics are met and to assess whether more cost-effective options may be available for new bidding or through internal staffing.

Indirect Allocations

Finally, it is important to note that finance assigns some expenses to surgical services as indirect expenses. These allocated expenses are from non-revenue-producing departments such as food services or security. Surgical services may be allocated a large portion of these expenses if they are distributed based on gross revenues or square feet. It is usually beneficial to separate indirect expenses from direct expenses in cost-management programs.

ACHIEVING OPTIMAL EXPENSE MANAGEMENT

Departments with the highest expenses will always attract the attention of finance departments to explore opportunities for reducing costs. The operating room is one of the most expensive departments to manage. Increasing efficiency, decreasing supply/implant costs, and reducing variations in clinical practice are methods widely used to achieve cost management in surgical services. Historical approaches to cost management have focused most heavily on managing staffing and supply/implant expenses.

Traditional Labor and Supply Chain Cost-Reduction Programs

Efforts to reduce staff expense have focused on improving efficiencies to streamline work processes, reducing non-value-added activities, modifying roles and responsibilities, and reducing the time patients are in the OR or perianesthesia units and the turnover time in between patients. This results in reducing the number of full-time equivalents (FTEs), reducing overtime paid, and reducing the use of temporary agency labor. Many organizations have achieved success with these approaches; the strategies and tactics for these are covered in Chapter 5.

Efforts to reduce supply and implant expenses have focused on attempts to minimize the number of vendors used to one or two preferred vendors. These standardization projects are often sponsored by supply chain departments but need to be fully supported by the surgical services department. Usually the standardization is based on a single product category or a group of products. Standardizing on bone cement is an example of a single product; surgical procedure packs would be an example of a vendor-based product. Many organizations have achieved some success with this approach but, as supplies and implants have changed, cost reductions have eroded and high costs have returned.

Supply and Implant Cost Management

There are three basic functions that drive the costs for supplies and implants. These are *selection*, *acquisition*, and *utilization*. Figure 4.3 shows the process and interaction of these three impacts.

Selection involves reviewing vendors and options in the medical supply market and engaging clinicians in a process to select the product most favored based on ease of use and desired outcome. Other considerations are vendor support for staff and physician training, and whether the product is included in a group-purchasing contract.

Acquisition is the process of negotiating the best price; the organization's purchasing department best accomplishes this. Department staff and physicians play a critical support role but are typically not involved in negotiating price.

Utilization (aka, usage) is how the product is used during procedures in conformance with contracted planned use and best practices to minimize waste and the total quantity consumed.

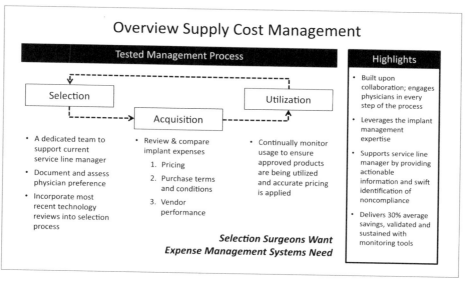

FIGURE 4.3 Sample Supply Cost Opportunity

Reducing Variations in Clinical Practice

A newer, improved approach to ongoing cost management involves forming multidisciplinary teams to review variation in all labor and nonlabor resource consumption for specific procedures or groups of similar procedures. For example, a project reviewing total hip procedures may be expanded to all total joint procedures.

Surgeons are often not aware of the resources and costs generated from their surgical procedures or those performed by colleagues. Raising this awareness with surgeons in a collaborative comparative analysis can help to identify opportunities to significantly reduce costs. Experience has shown that when this is done in a truly collaborative environment, with a commitment to meeting objectives without compromising quality outcomes, rapid success has been reported.

Multidisciplinary team membership typically includes surgeons, OR staff, supply chain, and finance. The group is formed with specific objectives that typically address managing quality of care outcomes; comparing staff use practices, instrumentation, supply and implants; and identifying variation that can be reduced or eliminated without reducing quality outcomes. Quality outcome measures are identified by the group early in the project. These measures are used as a comparison when reviewing products and used to track outcomes once standard agreements are implemented. For example, surgeons may be using different vendors for fracture management hardware (screws and plates implanted to stabilize a fracture for healing). Agreeing on outcome measures and reviewing data (e.g., unexpected return to OR, post-op complication data) brings objective data to the table for decisions on product selection.

Engaging surgeons is key to success. Surgeons are often not aware of the costs and resources used in their procedures. They also have not often taken part in a collaborative process with other surgeons, and the organization, to compare the use of resources and determine options that will not appreciably affect their practices. Figure 4.4 demonstrates a multiple surgeon comparison of resources used and opportunities to reduce expenses.

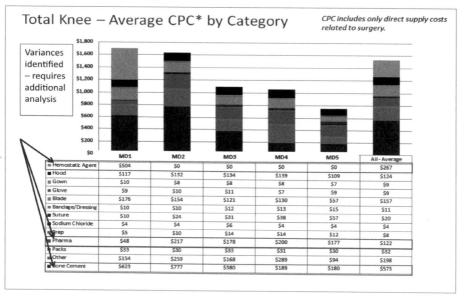

FIGURE 4.4   Analytics: Variations in Physician Preference Items

THE CAPITAL BUDGET

The capital budget process varies widely across organizations. Some organizations have extensive programs and processes to approve new capital; others manage capital allocation more informally.

Continual access to capital funding often dictates the extent of a healthcare organization's capital program. Organizations that have stable access to capital will often have a defined 1- to 3-year program and build multiple phases for request, review, and approval using multidisciplinary teams. These surgical services departments know their approved capital budget at the start of the fiscal year. Departments with less access to this information will minimize the time invested in more elaborate programs by gathering input from departments and key leaders. They will gather information on the best use of limited capital funds, capital item requests, and their priorities, but they will hold off on approval until funds are released throughout the year.

Surgical Services Capital Asset Management

The strength of any surgical program depends heavily on the state of its equipment and instrumentation. Requests for new or replacement equipment are constant, as the technology for performing surgery rapidly progresses. Meeting these needs and identifying priorities will be critical to success. In addition, current capital equipment has specific life cycles and requires a schedule of when to replace. Some equipment may be so old that available parts and repairs may not be possible. Achieving balance in understanding the priority for replacement of equipment versus acquiring new equipment is the best approach.

Despite the extent of an organization's capital budgeting program, every surgical services department needs to develop and maintain knowledge of the state of current equipment. Every equipment item has typically been logged by the biomedical department. That is the starting point for projecting equipment replacement needs based on frequency of use and life cycle. A 3- to 5-year replacement plan should be developed with input from staff and physicians.

In addition, a log of new capital equipment requests should be developed and sorted by surgical program or specialty. Some of this will overlap with the need for replacement of existing outdated equipment. New programs and the addition of new surgeons will drive the majority of new equipment requests. It is always helpful to gain input from staff and physicians in developing and prioritizing this list.

TYPICAL FINANCIAL MEASURES

There are wide ranges of potential financial measures that can be tracked and monitored to ensure the department is achieving solid fiscal performance. These should be internally and externally benchmarked. Among those that should be considered are:

- Total gross and net revenues
- Average revenue per case
- Average supply cost per case
- Worked hours per case minute
- Contribution margin
- Inventory value and turns per year
- Expenses by category of supply item
- Expenses per specialty
- Amount of bad debt write-off

EXECUTIVE LEADERSHIP LESSONS

- It is the responsibility of both executive leadership and the PEC to understand and monitor surgeon motivation in the purchase of equipment, supplies, and implantable devices. Equipment and supply expense is a significant driver of surgical revenue as well as quality clinical outcomes. Therefore, all purchases should be made in consideration of value provided, cost, and quality. Active leadership participation is required to drive outcomes that accommodate physician preference in a cost-effective manner.

- While most organizations create a budget based on last year's performance with a volume or expense adjustment, it is critically important to periodically perform a zero-based budget exercise. This will significantly improve confidence in the budget because it will reflect the continual improvements made in processes, the care model, physical plant improvements, and expense-reduction efforts.

- When projecting case volume, consider:

  - Market forces

  - Service line growth

  - Surgeon recruitment and attrition, including impending retirements

  - Technological improvements and payer changes, which may shift cases to alternate sites of care

- Contemporary technology, universal procedure rooms, and physician training and credentialing are blurring the lines between surgery, radiology, interventional radiology, and cardiology. Because this may lead to operational confusion with a potential impact on revenue, it is important to have these crucial conversations with physicians. Incentives must be aligned between and within departments, with a clear connection to the organization's strategic plan.

REFERENCES

American College of Surgeons (ACS). (2018). *Physicians as assistants at surgery: 2018 update.* Retrieved from https://www.facs.org/~/media/files/advocacy/pubs/2018_pas.ashx

American Society of PeriAnesthesia Nurses (ASPAN). 2017. *2017-2018 Perianesthesia Nursing Standards Practice Recommendations and Interpretive Statements:* Retrieved from https://www.aspan.org

Association of periOperative Registered Nurses (AORN). (2018). Standards of operating room staffing, Guidelines for Perioperative Practice. Retrieved from https://www.aornstandards.org

Centers for Medicare & Medicaid Services (CMS). (2018). *CY 2018 Medicare Physician Fee Schedule.* Retrieved from https://www.cms.gov

Childers, C., & Maggard-Gibbons, M. (2018). Understanding costs of care in the operating room. *JAMA Surgery.* Advance online publication. doi: 10.1001/jamasurg.2017.6233

Weiss, A. J., Elixhauser, A., & Andrews, R. M. (2014). *Characteristics of operating room procedures in U.S. hospitals, 2011.* Healthcare Cost and Utilization Project, Statistical Brief #170. Rockville, MD: Agency for Healthcare Research and Quality (AHRQ). Retrieved from https://hcup-us.ahrq.gov/reports/statbriefs/sb170-Operating-Room-Procedures-United-States-2011.jsp

PERFORMANCE
MANAGEMENT

Running an efficient and cost-effective surgical services program, and meeting surgeon expectations, are two of the greatest challenges surgical services leaders face each day.

Most CEOs will report that successful surgeon recruitment and retention depend on easy access to the surgery schedule. Surgeons want to be able to schedule cases whenever they choose. They need to accommodate their busy schedules, which often include office hours and performing cases at multiple hospitals and ambulatory centers. In addition, patients often request to have surgical procedures as soon as possible to accommodate their own busy schedules or to comply with insurance requirements such as annual deductible limits. To gain this flexibility, surgeons will often request to have personal reserved time available for scheduling cases. The problem is that many surgeons do not have a sufficient and steady caseload to be able to consistently, or reliably, fill a block of time. This catch-22 often leads to poor operating room (OR) utilization and even poorer staff productivity.

Surgical services department leaders are required to maintain high levels of operating room utilization as a means of achieving budgeted targets related to staff productivity, including employed or contracted physicians. Additionally, this is a critical metric in determining if the organization is achieving sufficient return on investment for the physical facility, including costly capital equipment. Leaders need to understand the myriad of dynamics that drive resource utilization and the effective tactics for managing surgeon demand, facilitating their convenient access to the schedule. Managers face the operational challenges of this complex and resource-intense environment, optimizing the preferences of multiple providers and consumers within a financially constrained model of care.

Attaining the highest levels of performance and achieving the best clinical outcomes requires the effective management and synchronicity of a wide range of systems and processes, technology dependencies, and personnel dynamics. Key performance measures reflect the effectiveness of thoughtful policies and processes—which provide clear lines of authority and accountability for managers and staff alike. Careful ongoing assessments of these interactions need to be well understood and closely monitored to ensure that decisions will improve outcomes and achieve program objectives, while avoiding unintended consequences.

THE OR SCHEDULE: THE BACKBONE OF EFFICIENCY

Surgical case scheduling is one of the key interactions that drives all subsequent outcome measures. The OR scheduling system is the foundation for achieving the most effective and efficient performance and the highest levels of physician, staff, and patient satisfaction.

A well-functioning scheduling process is a major factor in providing surgeons with access to schedule patients, and it lays the groundwork for the avoidance of unnecessary delays. Ultimately, the goal is the optimal use of all resources including staff, rooms, and equipment. A poor system, on the other hand, has the potential to generate significant dissatisfaction, resulting in the inefficient use of resources despite any and all attempts to improve throughput and performance.

A review of the scheduling process and the various options for effective management will be helpful in understanding how to arrive at the best performance outcomes. The OR scheduling system fundamentally consists of two elements or subprocesses: schedule planning and schedule management.

Schedule Planning

To successfully manage the schedule, it is critical that the schedule is actually achievable. Wishful thinking, or placating a frustrated surgeon by burdening the schedule with an impractical addition, can undermine resource utilization and delay other surgeons as they manage their time. This process requires data-driven, well-thought-out and well-designed scheduling guidelines that meet surgeon practice demands and provide for the placement and sequencing of cases, incrementally, over several weeks. If the plan is not realistic, no amount of scheduling management will correct for the delays that will occur.

The fundamental elements of schedule planning include the policies, procedures, and guidelines for scheduling a surgical case. This begins with establishing the OR hours of operation for elective, add-on, and emergency cases. The hours of operation are specified by day of the week and available operating hours for each day. The plan should also identify which hours are available for elective surgical cases and those for add-on urgent and emergent cases. Typically these are called the *resource hours* for the operating room. These resource hours reflect when the organization will have nursing and anesthesia staff, as well as equipment, supplies, and instrument resources available to perform cases. After the resource hours are established, block time needs to be assigned and distributed across surgical specialties, or services, and individual surgeons looking to reserve time for scheduling elective cases. The objective is to reserve time within the elective resource hours so that surgeons with a high volume of cases can easily schedule patients days and even weeks prior to the day of surgery. Once these hours and block time are established, rules or guidelines are stipulated to direct the scheduling of cases.

Establishing Resource Hours

Deciding how many resource hours to make available each day for scheduling cases and assigning block time will drive the ability to meet the highest levels of room utilization and staff productivity. Typically, elective hours are set from 7:00 a.m. to 3:30 p.m. daily. Many organizations will extend these elective case hours for a smaller number of rooms, typically until 5:00, 7:00, and even 9:00 p.m. This will allow the organization to accommodate longer cases or higher volumes each day and to expand the available resource hours for elective cases. This vertical expansion is needed when surgical case volume demand exceeds the number of operating rooms available. Additionally, room availability and the hours each room is open may be determined by day of the week. For example, the demand for scheduling cases may dip on Fridays. Therefore, fewer rooms will be required. In contrast, resource hours may be added on Mondays, which have a higher demand resulting from weekend inpatient admissions.

The numbers of available rooms and hours are planned based on projected case volume and targeted utilization, along with the resources required for an actual or budgeted caseload.

The first step in establishing resource hours is to convert projected case volume to total case minutes for each surgical specialty or surgeon. This is done by multiplying the number of cases by the average case time for each surgical specialty or surgeon. This calculation is made for different types of cases within every surgical specialty, thereby accounting for varying levels of intensity. Targeted utilization is typically established to reflect industry best practices. There is no clear authority that has established what the industry best practice for utilization is. Healthcare consulting groups have recommended utilization rates at 80%–85%. Several professional organizations, including the Health Finance Management Association, the American Society of Anesthesiologists, and AORN have concurred that 80% utilization is high-performing efficiency (Fixler & Wright, 2013). For most organizations, this utilization rate is between 75% and 80%. Utilization is calculated as:

Total Case Minutes + Turnover Time/Total Resource Hours × 100%

It is important to note that the targeted utilization rate of 75%–80% is used for elective hours of operation. Utilization rates for add-on and emergency-case hours are much lower due to the unpredictability of these cases. For example, targeted utilization rates for the evening shift hours would range from 70% to 40% as the evening progresses. In addition, if the organization is expanding case volume, utilization rates are often set at lower rates for short periods of time. For example, experience has shown that rates might be set at 60% for 3 to 4 months to provide more open time for new volume to be scheduled.

Assigning Block Time

Blocks of elective time are usually assigned, or reserved, for different days of the week and hours of the day to allow for better surgeon access to the schedule. Typically, this block time is distributed to a surgeon, groups of surgeons, or a surgical specialty. A small amount of "open" block time, typically 10%–20% of overall elective resource hours, is reserved to allow for surgeons without block time to schedule a case, or for unexpected add-on or emergent cases. This allows surgeons to plan office hours and other nonsurgical case time activity, including rounding and administrative responsibilities, around their planned surgical block times.

Block time must be assigned and managed to meet a targeted utilization rate similar to the overall hours of operation. These rates are calculated by utilizing the same formulas and methodologies. Most organizations expect the surgeon-assigned block times to mirror the overall targeted utilization rate. So, the expected block time utilization rate would be 75% if the overall target utilization rate is 75%.

Some organizations have historically assigned lower expectations for block time utilization, believing that unused block time would be filled with add-on cases. Industry experience has shown this does not occur, so organizations that do this are setting themselves up for failure in meeting overall utilization rates. Block assignments are typically made for high-volume surgeons demonstrating consistent and predictable case volumes. These blocks of time are typically granted in 4- or 8-hour increments.

Industry studies demonstrate that 8-hour blocks are the most efficient because they eliminate the transition of block users on a given day. These transitions are often affected by earlier delays in case progression, thus making the start of the second 4-hour block less predictable.

Because of the potential to be impacted by delays, many surgeons view these afternoon blocks as less desirable and, consequently, organizations have difficulties filling them. One tactic to filling these afternoon blocks is to "guarantee" the start time by closing the scheduling of elective time for one hour before the start of the afternoon block, thus allowing a cushion of time in case the last case of the morning block runs late.

Most organizations have some block matrix already established.

If surgeons wish to make a change to the established block matrix (e.g., requesting initial or additional block time), they would do so in writing, typically using a standard format request document that outlines the process and indicates the expected utilization and release process. Key elements on the form should include:

- Request for individual or shared block
- Specific day of week and hours of the day
- Frequency of the block, for example every week or first week of the month, etc.
- Estimated number of cases and case time per month

Organizations will often work with groups of surgeons to establish shared blocks of time (see Figure 5.1). This can be particularly helpful when surgeons do not have enough volume to sustain a block of time themselves but share the same, or a similar, surgical specialty. Group scheduling also supports the organization's ability to provide competent staff, equipment, and instrumentation for each surgical specialty. This specialization of staff is reviewed in Chapter 6, "Nursing Management in Surgical Services." The surgeons within the block designate who will have first or subsequent priority; this priority may change from week to week.

	MONDAY	TUESDAY
WEEK **1**	2 CLOSED 3 CLOSED 4 BARIATRICS 6 Dr. A 7 OPEN 8 ORTHO 9 ORTHO	2 CLOSED 3 GENERAL / OPEN 4 BARIATRICS 6 ENT 7 GYN 8 ORTHO 9 ORTHO
WEEK **2**	2 CLOSED 3 CLOSED 4 BARIATRICS 6 Dr. A / OPEN 7 F & D 8 ORTHO 9 ORTHO	2 CLOSED 3 GENERAL / OPEN 4 BARIATRICS 6 ENT 7 GYN 8 ORTHO 9 ORTHO
WEEK **3**	2 CLOSED 3 OPEN 4 BARIATRICS 6 Dr. A 7 ORTHO 8 ORTHO 9 ORTHO	2 CLOSED 3 GENERAL / OPEN 4 BARIATRICS 6 ENT 7 GYN 8 ORTHO 9 ORTHO
WEEK **4**	2 CLOSED 3 OPEN 4 BARIATRICS 6 DR. A 7 F & D 8 ORTHO 9 ORTHO	2 CLOSED 3 GENERAL / OPEN 4 BARIATRICS 6 ENT 7 GYN 8 ORTHO 9 ORTHO
WEEK **5**	2 CLOSED 3 CLOSED 4 BARIATRICS 6 OPEN 7 DR. B 8 CLOSED 9 Dr. S	2 CLOSED 3 DR. C / OPEN 4 BARIATRICS 6 OPEN 7 DR. D 8 DR. E 9 DR. E

WEDNESDAY	THURSDAY	FRIDAY
2 CLOSED	2 CLOSED	2 CLOSED
3 GENERAL / CLOSED	3 GENERAL	3 CLOSED
4 PLASTICS	4 GYN	4 PLASITCS / OPEN
6 ENT / OPEN	6 ENT	6 ENT / OPEN
7 GU / OPEN	7 GU / OPEN	7 GU / OPEN
8 ORTHO	8 ORTHO	8 ORTHO
9 ORTHO	9 OPEN	9 OPEN

2 CLOSED	2 CLOSED	2 CLOSED
3 GENERAL / CLOSED	3 GENERAL	3 CLOSED
4 PLASTICS	4 GYN	4 PLASITCS / OPEN
6 ENT / OPEN	6 ENT	6 ENT / OPEN
7 GU / OPEN	7 GU / OPEN	7 GU / OPEN
8 ORTHO	8 ORTHO	8 ORTHO
9 ORTHO	9 OPEN	9 OPEN

2 CLOSED	2 CLOSED	2 CLOSED
3 GENERAL / CLOSED	3 GENERAL	3 CLOSED
4 PLASTICS	4 GYN	4 PLASITCS / OPEN
6 ENT / OPEN	6 ENT	6 ENT / OPEN
7 GU / OPEN	7 GU / OPEN	7 GU / OPEN
8 ORTHO	8 ORTHO	8 ORTHO
9 ORTHO	9 OPEN	9 OPEN

2 CLOSED	2 CLOSED	2 CLOSED
3 GENERAL / CLOSED	3 GENERAL	3 CLOSED
4 PLASTICS	4 GYN	4 PLASITCS / OPEN
6 ENT / OPEN	6 ENT	6 ENT / OPEN
7 GU / OPEN	7 GU / OPEN	7 GU / OPEN
8 ORTHO	8 ORTHO	8 ORTHO
9 ORTHO	9 OPEN	9 OPEN

2 CLOSED	2 CLOSED	2 CLOSED
3 DR. F / OPEN	3 DR. H	3 CLOSED
4 DR. G	4 DR. I	4 DR. K
6 OPEN	6 OPEN	6 OPEN
7 DR. B	7 OPEN	7 OPEN
8 DR. E	8 DR. J	8 OPEN
9 DR. E	9 OPEN	9 DR. L

FIGURE 5.1 Sample Block Grid

A common practice is to allow block owners to release their block time if it is not needed, thereby allowing other surgeons access to this time. These release times are based on the pattern of referrals or consults from primary care physicians to a surgeon. Some patients may need elective surgery within 48 hours, while others could wait a week or more. Most surgical specialties see patients at least a week, or more, in advance of their scheduled surgeries; consequently, release times for these specialties are typically set 5 business days, or more, in advance of the day of surgery.

Some specialties may experience more urgent elective referrals (e.g., vascular surgery); therefore, release times for these specialties are set lower, typically at 1 to 2 days. A surgeon also may release their time while on vacation or attending conferences. A minimum of 60 to 90 days is required to release block time to other surgeons to allow other surgeons to schedule their cases into this released time. A good practice is to have the OR schedulers notify other surgeons' offices when a block time is released. Ultimately, the release of these blocks allows for improved block and overall room utilization.

Block time utilization requires continual management and oversight as a means of ensuring the most effective distribution of time. Adjustments need to be made if blocks are not consistently meeting targeted utilization rates or, by contrast, if they are exceeding the utilization rate. The scheduling guidelines should include a section addressing block time management that details the process for assignment and adjustment of block time. In addition, the guidelines should define the block time monitoring and adjustment process.

All surgeons and relevant staff should be made aware of the guidelines and methodology for measuring outcomes. Block time utilization should be monitored every month and adjusted on a quarterly basis if required. Notification in writing (and preferably a verbal touch base as well) should be sent to block owners if there is a significant drop below targeted utilization for any one month, thereby preparing for the quarterly adjustment.

GROUPING BLOCKS BASED ON LEVEL OF UTILIZATION

Chances are your organization has already granted blocks and is struggling with varying levels of utilization with no effective strategy to redistribute the block time. To get started, a good approach is to group the blocks into ranges of utilization rates and then take appropriate actions based on the level of utilization. For instance:

- Less than 30%: remove block time and offer open time to schedule cases
- 30%–70%: curtail the amount of block time to increase block utilization rate
- 70% or greater: usually organizations do not take actions outside of continual monitoring

The perioperative executive committee (PEC) manages block time with input from the surgeon advisory group (SAG). The PEC may establish a block utilization committee to conduct the deep analysis and make recommendations for changes or assignments of block time to the PEC. It is key to include discussion with the surgeons involved to improve understanding of the process and to take into account various factors when considering these metrics. Some examples are:

- Process for eliminating or reducing block time for low utilizers
- Reasonable block release times so that other surgeons can utilize this time
- Flexible and rotating priorities for surgeons sharing a block

SURGICAL SCHEDULE MANAGEMENT

Organizations often have outdated and vague scheduling policies, procedures, and block scheduling guidelines. This contributes to the confusion around scheduling, leading to surgeon dissatisfaction and poor utilization. The surgical department medical staff often develop these documents with little consideration for the organization's targets of performance. The surgical service department leadership may have developed them without executive guidance or sufficient surgeon participation. Processes for updating and revising these documents may not be clear or may be too cumbersome to make changes. Clear and concise documents serve as the foundation for achieving high utilization and productivity while maintaining high surgeon and patient satisfaction.

Industry best practice demonstrates the merger and consolidation of these related documents into a comprehensive set of scheduling guidelines. These guidelines include:

- Targets or utilization and resource hours
- The process and requirements for scheduling cases
- The responsibilities and actions that take place in managing the schedule
- Descriptions of the distribution and management of block and open time

Utilization Targets and Resource Hours

- List of the number of rooms and hours that are planned and staffed for elective and add-on cases. These add-on cases may be elective, urgent, or emergent.

- Targeted overall utilization rate and measures of efficiencies (e.g., on-time and turnover rates)

- Expectations for patient arrival times and targeted times needed for:

  - Pre-op admission and preparation of patients

  - Anesthesia pre-op evaluation

  - Surgeon arrival times to see patients, mark the operative site, and obtain consents if necessary

Process and Requirements for Scheduling Cases

- Process for requests to schedule an elective case, and any urgent or emergent cases

- Operating definitions for urgent and emergent cases, along with the process for assigning patients to a room

- Clearly identified target times for how soon urgent and emergent cases need to be started and, when necessary, what elective cases would be "bumped" or postponed.

- List of the detailed information that the surgeon or surgeon's office must provide to schedule a case, including:

  - Patient identifiers and contact information

  - Exact surgical procedure to be performed

  - Special requirements regarding the patient or materials needed for the case

Managing the Schedule

- Clear responsibilities are delineated for who manages the schedule and how any problems are resolved. This is often a shared responsibility, with nursing and anesthesia making decisions collaboratively.

- Process for bumping a case including communication, escalation, measure, and monitoring.

- Process for escalating the decision to the surgeon medical director, if the surgeon is not satisfied.

Block Time Management

- Guidelines for requesting and assigning blocks of time along with expectations to meet utilization targets. These block utilization targets are often a direct reflection of the overall utilization target. The ongoing process of how block utilization is monitored, with any resultant adjustments, also is delineated to avoid confusion.

- Assigned blocks often are released if cases are not scheduled within a period of 2 to 10 days, depending on the specialty. Once released, the block becomes open for anyone to schedule into. Blocks also may be released months in advance if surgeons are away at conferences or on vacation.

- The targeted amount of open and unblocked time is identified for surgeons who do not have a block time assigned. Best practice suggests this time be about 20% of the overall elective resource hours. Open block time is filled on a first-requested, first-scheduled basis.

Detailed surgical scheduling guidelines can be found in Appendix A. Figure 5.2 depicts a portion of the guidelines pertaining to release of block time.

4. BLOCK TIME UTILIZATION

4.1. Block time utilization is calculated by:

(Case Time + Turnover) / (Allocated time) = Utilization

4.1.1. Block time utilization will be monitored monthly and adjusted as needed to meet targets. The PEC will formally review on a semi-annual basis.

4.1.2. Surgical and turnover time adjacent to the allocated block time will be used for the calculation of the utilization.

4.1.3. Surgical and turnover time used outside of the block time will be reported as total time out of block.

4.1.4. Assigned blocks may be released by the specialty or surgeon by notice to the OR scheduling office but will remain part of the block utilization calculation.

4.1.5. A separate monitor for released blocked time will be maintained if blocks are repeatedly released (if affecting the block utilization assigned).

4.1.6. Other aspects considered in the review of block utilization will include:

- Chronic lateness

- Overbooking

- Booking phantom patients to hold block time

- Chronic cancellation of cases

- Chronic release of block time 7 business days in advance

- Nonpreventable cancellations

FIGURE 5.2 Sample Scheduling Guidelines

Managing Surgeon Demand

Getting surgeons involved early in the scheduling process, and having them review relevant data, is critical in achieving high levels of surgeon satisfaction. Difficulties in meeting surgeon needs and requests can be minimized when organizations have established sound scheduling guidelines and a good plan for distribution. In fact, industry best practice focuses on working closely with surgeons to develop scheduling guidelines, managing assigned blocks of operating room time, and managing open time that nonblock surgeons can use.

The process of effectively managing demand starts by working with a select group of surgeons to study scheduling practices and the historical, current, and projected utilization for each of the surgical specialties, groups of surgeons, and individual surgeons. Typically, a subcommittee of the perioperative executive committee (PEC, see Chapter 2, "Governance and Managing Resources") is formed, with some members of the SAG also participating.

Once a recommended block distribution plan is designed and approved by the PEC, work begins with individual surgical specialties, groups of surgeons, or individual surgeons. It is of paramount importance that surgical service leaders state the desire to meet surgeon requests at the beginning and the end of these meetings. In addition, the plan should present the required targets of utilization and the reasons the organization must achieve them.

Throughout this process and ensuing discussions, surgical services leaders should be genuine and open to any suggested modifications requested by the surgeons. They should accept suggestions that might work and commit to get back to the surgeons, following up in a timely manner. If a suggestion is not possible, this should be communicated immediately, along with an explanation of why the request cannot be accommodated. Finally, it's important to communicate that the process of reviewing surgeon caseload and utilization of block time is ongoing, will be closely monitored, and any required revisions will be made.

BALANCING SURGEON DEMAND WITH SOLID UTILIZATION

Several tactics can be used to meet surgeon demands and achieve solid utilization. Among the most successful are:

- Vary the hours of operations for elective surgery by different days of the week. Often there is a higher demand for surgery early in the week, especially for inpatient surgical cases such as orthopedics, spine, and neurosurgery. Opening more 10- and 12-hour rooms on these days, and leaving the others at 8 hours, will help to meet this demand; 10- and 12-hour shifts for staffing are then aligned with these days.

- Distribute blocks differently each week for surgeons who can't fill a block of time every week. For example, ENT may be given the first and third Wednesdays of the month; another similar service, like plastics, can be assigned the alternate second and third Wednesdays of the month.

- Assign a block of time to more than one surgeon to share the block. Develop the priority of which surgeons get the primary or secondary choice. This priority assignment can be rotated.

DAILY SCHEDULE MANAGEMENT

Establishing sound daily processes and responsibilities is crucial to ensure that scheduling guidelines are consistently followed and are enforced fairly and equitably. Scheduling coordinators from both nursing and anesthesia should be assigned to manage the schedule in a minute-by-minute process. These two leaders, working in collaboration, are critical to achieving an effective scheduling success. They must possess skills to coordinate multiple details as well as the ability to communicate effectively in what are often tense situations. These leaders often are positioned at the OR control desk to receive calls for add-on cases or to notify members of the surgical team of schedule changes. The leaders also are responsible for communicating with the preoperative and postoperative patient care units, as well as with support departments such as radiology. Changes to the schedule need to be coordinated and confirmed so that interdependent units and departments can accommodate the changes and continually optimize their internal systems and processes. They also need to conduct rounds of the OR suites to maintain situational awareness and to monitor the progress of cases.

Typically, adjusted average case times are used for setting case times on the OR schedule. The actual length of the case will vary and will require close monitoring to ensure the next patients and staff are ready to follow the preceding case. In some circumstances, cases may run over the scheduled time; the next cases may need to be moved to another OR suite to remain on schedule.

Audio-visual technology is developing, allowing remote monitoring of the OR suites. Cameras are set up in each OR suite, and monitors are located at the OR control desk to allow for visual reviews of the progress of a case. However, early use of this technology still supports the need for rounding in the OR to enable face-to-face communication (Saver, 2017).

TIPS FOR SUCCESSFUL SCHEDULE MANAGEMENT

- **Daily caseload management huddles or "look-aheads."** Leaders of daily caseload management should review the next day's schedule and optimize the flow of cases while ensuring that each patient care unit and support department is well coordinated. This single tactic has allowed surgical services departments to achieve marked improvement in utilization, on-time, and turnover time rates. Caseload management huddles typically occur between 10:00 and 11:00 a.m., for 15 to 20 minutes, and include managers from scheduling, the OR, preadmission, pre- and post-op units, sterile processing, and the nursing and anesthesia control desk coordinators. Before the schedule closes, any problems with the schedule, patient preparation, or instrumentation/equipment are resolved to ensure a more efficient use of resources and throughput. In addition to looking at the next day's schedule, the team often reviews how well the day started, noting any problems with on-time starts while fresh in everyone's minds. As the team becomes more efficient with the huddle, it will frequently look ahead to the following 2 to 5 days of scheduling.

- **Early morning review of changes.** Early morning activities are crucial to getting started. The OR nursing and anesthesia coordinators should review any add-ons or requests to change the schedule that may have been posted overnight. These coordinators should then check in with the preoperative unit leader to communicate any schedule changes or to identify if any patients are arriving late.

- **Continued monitoring.** Monitoring should continue throughout the day, especially because unexpected changes may impact the schedule and cause delays. The postoperative units also should be included as the day progresses to plan for receiving patients from the OR and discharging inpatients to hospital units.

KEY PERFORMANCE INDICATORS IN SURGICAL SERVICES

High-performing organizations set strategies to ensure that surgical services are performing at the highest possible levels. The following questions and related probes can help ensure high quality:

- Are the operating room and related departments efficient?

- How do my quality outcomes compare with other organizations?

- Can I improve vital contribution margin by focusing all attention on improving throughput and productivity?

- What are the key measures of performance that I should be tracking?

In recent years, more than 100 articles have been published addressing these questions and delving deeper into the identification of the most effective measures. In recognition of the importance of focusing on this area, some hospital C-suite executives have the improvement of certain OR performance measures built into their own annual goals.

It is a well-known management principle that gathering and using data for decision-making is crucial to success. Historically, however, surgical services leaders have been lacking in access to data and the ability to build reports that provided actionable information. Analysis had been done by pulling data from various disconnected systems such as OR scheduling, materials management, finance, and even manual throughput logs. Data was then entered in home-produced spreadsheets to generate performance information. Scarcity of detail and multiple errors resulted in a lack of trust in these reporting tools, leaving surgical services leaders to make decisions based on experience and intuition.

Fortunately, with the advent of the automated patient record and decision-support software integrated with OR scheduling, materials management, and finance systems, many surgical services departments now have access to reports that allow for improved resource management decision-making. National organizations like the American Society of Anesthesiologists (ASA) and the OR Benchmarks Collaborative (ORBC) have worked together to establish common definitions and formulas for computing data. Standard key productivity indicators are being monitored; these indicators can be compared internally, for progress, and externally, for benchmarking performance.

Following is a review of these key measures, with additional information to assist with interpretation. Financial measures are discussed at length in Chapter 4, "Budget and Financial Management."

OR Efficiency Measures

Operating Room Utilization

- *Operating room utilization* is the customary measure that conveys the efficiency of an OR. It is a simple calculation of the total time a patient is in an operating suite, plus case set-up time, divided by the total resource hours planned. Typically, it is calculated for elective hours of operation during daytime hours because these are considered "prime time" and highly desirable for scheduling elective cases. Resource hours should be a direct reflection of nursing shift times. Industry best practice reports utilization to be in the 80%–85% range.

- **Cautions:** Some organizations confuse operating room utilization with *block utilization* and only look at the expected start times of a block. However, this misrepresents the total time the OR is actually staffed. Also, keep in mind that utilization can never reach 100%, as 30 minutes is usually needed to open an OR suite at the beginning of the day, and at least 15 minutes is needed to properly close it down after the last case of the day. This accounts for about 10% of unused time over an 8-hour day. The remaining unused time represents some unpredictable unused time at the end of a day. For example, the last case of the day in an operating room may end at 3:15, with not enough time left after the 3:30 ending time to do another case. Even with high levels of utilization, a department may not be efficient if it experiences delays due to keeping patients in the OR for a longer than average time.

First Case On-Time Performance

- *First case on-time performance* is typically monitored based on the first case of the day. This eliminates multiple delays that may occur for subsequent cases. First case on-time performance is a critical indicator as it sets the tone for efficiency throughout the rest of the day. Industry best practice reports first case on-time rates to be in the 90%–95% range.

- **Cautions:** Some organizations build in a small grace period of 5 to 10 minutes and report these cases as on time. This is an outdated practice that was originally used to correct for variation of clocks in each operating room. With automated time capture through EHRs, this is no longer necessary.

Turnover Time

- A significant efficiency measure, *turnover time* and first case on-time starts are the most important measures for surgeons, as they view these as primary indicators of delays during the operating day. Time in the OR is critical to surgeons, who also need to spend time out of the OR to see patients and grow their practices. Turnover time is defined as the time between cases, starting with the patient out of the room, and ending with the next patient entering the room. Turnover time is calculated as an average for all cases; it also may be broken down to individual surgical specialties, or groups, to limit variability. More complex cases (e.g., cardiac, total joints or spine) may take longer for cleaning the room and preparing for the next case than simpler cases (e.g., biopsies or eye cases). Industry best practice for turnover rates ranges from 10 minutes for simple cases to as much as 40 minutes for the most complex cases. Most hospitals target an overall average of 25 to 30 minutes.

■ **Cautions:** Care must be taken to not count unscheduled and unused time between cases as turnover time. This unscheduled and unused time typically occurs when the room is switched to a different surgeon or when the morning block is not fully scheduled with cases. These gaps in the schedule, which may skew actual turnover time, can often be eliminated from the calculation by discarding this gap of time, which would be mistaken for turnover time. One tactic to identify these unscheduled gaps is to identify cases with turnover times greater than 60 minutes. If the unscheduled time is confirmed, then this gap time is not included in calculating the turnover rate.

Case Interval Time Measures

■ *Case interval time measures* are quickly becoming the preferred way to evaluate utilization (Foster, 2012). These measures divide out the times for significant milestones in the operating room that represent the progress of a case, and they are inclusive of the entire patient encounter in the operating room. Case interval time measures include: the time between when a patient enters the room to the incision; the time between when a patient enters the room to anesthesia induction; the actual procedure time between the incision to the end of the procedure; and from the end of the procedure to when the patient leaves the room.

- These time intervals indicate how efficient the process is within the OR suite and provide valuable information regarding any delays that might occur after the patient enters the room.

Case Cancellations

- Case cancellations create delays, especially if they occur on the day of surgery. These rates should be minimal, with less than 5% occurring on the day of surgery.

Accurate Case Scheduled and Case Duration

- Case scheduling accuracy and case duration are additional efficiency measures that are gaining in popularity. Delays can occur if the full details of the procedure being performed aren't identified in the scheduling of the case. This is informally known as "truth in scheduling." Accurate scheduling of a procedure allows for all members of the surgical services team to plan the needed resources for a specific case. In addition, under- or overestimating time planned for a case will create delays for cases that follow. Organizations are targeting 100% of accurate cases scheduled, with no more than 15 minutes (give or take) for accuracy of case duration.

Perianesthesia Efficiency Measures

Preadmission Screening and Patient Preparation

Preadmission screening and preparation of patients by nursing and anesthesia will ensure timely admission on the day of surgery and reduce cancellations due to unexpected clinical conditions that can be identified and corrected before the day of surgery. The industry standard is 100% screening of patients. Preadmission screening should be monitored as consistently as other measures.

In addition to preadmission screening, patient preparation involves ensuring that operative consents and surgeon history and physicals are completed before the day of surgery because these take up valuable time if obtained on the day of surgery. Once again, the industry standard is to obtain 100% of these before the day of admission.

Throughput Measures

Throughput measures look at the average length of stay on the preoperative and postoperative units and are additional indicators of delays. These measures, in particular, have a significant effect on patient satisfaction. Measures include: admission to OR time, primary recovery room average length of stay, and admission-to-discharge time for outpatients.

Quality Measures

Quality measures include:

- Patient satisfaction
- Return to OR after the procedure is completed
- Readmission rates

- Infection rates

- Other complication rates

DASHBOARDS AND BENCHMARKING

Every surgical services department should have a consolidated dash-board of key performance measures. The dashboard should include the standard measures as covered earlier in this chapter. Additional measures should encompass specific items from the department's current performance-improvement projects. For example, if the goal is to target case accuracy improvement, an additional measure would be to compare scheduled case time to actual case time.

Dashboards should include comparisons to internal and external benchmarks to gauge the progress and success of the department. Internal benchmarks track progress over time within the organization and are used most often for setting annual objectives for performance improvement. Dashboards may compare performance between surgical specialty practices, creating some natural competition. Dashboards also may report performance against external benchmarks obtained from industry sources. When using external benchmarks, it is critical to use a closely comparative group to avoid challenges from physicians and staff.

In addition to the department's dashboard, individual surgeon score-cards are now being generated to understand differences in surgeon-to-surgeon performance, identify trends, and provide surgeons more detailed information, with a focus on their case volume. Figure 5.3 provides an example of a surgeon-specific scorecard.

Volumes				
Patient Type	Case Count	%	6-Month Total	6-Month %
Inpatient	24	92%	132	88%
Outpatient	2	8%	18	12%
Total	26	100%	150	100%

Surgeon 1 Volume

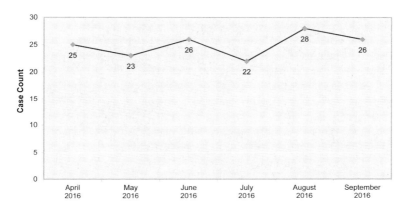

Block Utilization							
Block Name	Scheduled Minutes	Released Minutes	Available Minutes	During Block Minutes	Out of Block Minutes	Total Surgical Minutes	Block Utilization
Surgeon 1	3600	0	3600	2150	450	3350	60%
GEN Group	1680	0	1680	980	1816	3223	58%

Surgeon 1 Block Utilization

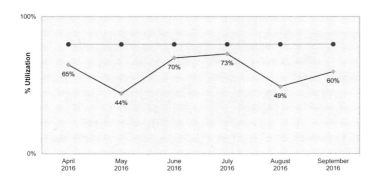

FIGURE 5.3   SHC020 Surgeon Scorecard—U.S. Sample
Used with permission from Sullivan Healthcare Consulting

111

EXECUTIVE LEADERSHIP LESSONS

- The availability of surgical schedule time and the efficiency of the scheduling process are key drivers in surgeon recruitment. The measurement and monitoring of process and outcome metrics related to the surgical schedule and utilization are crucial leadership responsibilities.

- Managing surgical services requires the concurrent optimization of customer and physician scheduling preferences, maximizing facility and personnel utilization, and having safe processes, all while achieving a maximum return on investment.

- The OR scheduling system fundamentally consists of two elements or subprocesses: schedule planning and schedule management.

- An effective scheduling process requires data-driven, well-thought-out and well-designed scheduling guidelines that meet surgeon practice demands and provide for the placement and sequencing of cases, incrementally, over several weeks. If the plan is not realistic, no amount of scheduling management will correct for the delays that will occur.

- In collaboration with the PEC, it is the surgical services leader's responsibility to establish the resource hours, or hours by day of the week, they will have resources (personnel, facility, and equipment) available for surgical cases.

- Utilization is calculated as: Total Case Minutes + Turnover Time/Total Resource Hours x 100%.

- Blocks of elective time are usually assigned or reserved for different days of the week and hours of the day to allow for better surgeon access to the schedule. A small amount of "open" block time, typically 10%–20% of overall elective resource hours, is reserved to allow for surgeons without block time to schedule a case or for unexpected add-on or emergent cases. This allows surgeons to plan office hours and other nonsurgical case time activity, including rounding and administrative responsibilities, around their planned surgical block times.

- Surgeon utilization of block time is typically set at the overall OR utilization rate. For example, if you have set the overall OR utilization target at 75%, then you will expect each surgeon with assigned block time to achieve 75% utilization. If a surgeon currently splits cases between several organizations, assigning block time and encouraging efficient utilization may facilitate a shift in the market as a surgeon weighs the convenience of set schedule availability.

- Many organizations historically assigned lower expectations for block time utilization, believing that unused block time would be filled with add-on cases. Industry experience has shown this does not occur, and organizations set themselves up for failure in meeting overall utilization rates.

- Organizations will often work with groups of surgeons to establish shared blocks of time. This can be particularly helpful when surgeons do not have enough volume to sustain a block of time themselves but share the same, or a similar, surgical specialty. Group scheduling also supports the organization's ability to provide competent staff, equipment, and instrumentation for each surgical specialty.

- Most surgical specialties see patients at least a week or more in advance of their scheduled surgeries; consequently, release times for these specialties are typically set 5 or more business days in advance of the day of surgery.

- Quick reference for adjusting block time:

  - Less than 30%: remove block time and offer open time to schedule cases

  - 30%–70%: curtail the amount of block time to increase block utilization rate

  - 70% or greater: usually organizations do not take actions outside of continual monitoring

- Organizations often have outdated and vague scheduling policies, procedures, and block scheduling guidelines. This contributes to the confusion around scheduling, leading to surgeon dissatisfaction and poor utilization.

- Industry best practice focuses on working closely with surgeons to develop scheduling guidelines, managing assigned blocks of operating room time, and managing open time that nonblock surgeons can use.

- Executives and surgeon leaders should work closely with surgeons in using data to drive utilization conversations. They should accept suggestions that might work and commit to getting back to the surgeons in a timely manner. If a particular suggestion is not possible, communicate immediately, offering an explanation of why the request cannot be accommodated.

REFERENCES

Fixler, T., & Wright, J. G. (2013). Identification and use of operating room efficiency indicators: The problem of definition. *Canadian Journal of Surgery, 56*(4), 224–226. doi: 10.1503/cjs.020712. Retrieved from https://www.ncbi.nlm.nih.gov/pmc/articles/PMC3728239/

Foster, T. (2012, January). Data for benchmarking your OR's performance. *OR Manager, 28*(1). Retrieved from https://www.ormanager.com/wp-content/uploads/2012/01/0112_ORM_5.Benchmark_r.pdf

Saver, C. (2017, December). Remote video auditing: A path to compliance and safety. *OR Manager, 33*(12). Retrieved from https://arrowsight.com/public/as/pdf/OR%20Manager%20-%20Remote%20Video%20Auditing%20-%20A%20Path%20to%20Compliance%20and%20Safety.pdf

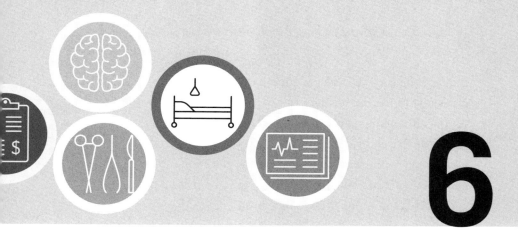

6

NURSING MANAGEMENT IN SURGICAL SERVICES

One of the first challenges the new executive will face is the recruitment and retention of an adequate number of highly competent clinical staff capable of providing increasingly complex surgical care and confidently participating as members of the care team. High vacancy rates and long training times create dependency on expensive travel nurses in many organizations. Experienced staff are finding themselves more and more taxed by excessive overtime. Surgeons are increasingly demanding better training for operating room (OR) staff because they prefer a specialty team or specific staff available for their cases. In addition, finance departments may be looking for ways to reduce overall staff FTEs (full-time equivalents) without completely understanding the factors driving the required number of FTEs or the rising costs for travel nurses and premium pay.

Staffing the surgical services areas has become increasingly difficult, especially in the recruitment of experienced OR nurses. Predictions for overall nursing shortages have ebbed and flowed for over 20 years, primarily driven by demographics and the expansion of opportunities for women in the workforce beyond the traditional roles of teaching and nursing. These nursing shortages have contributed to a rise in vacancy rates and unique difficulties in sourcing OR nurses and surgical technicians (Patterson, 2012). In addition to recruiting new candidates, surgical service leaders are challenged with the looming retirement of many in the current nursing workforce. A significant percentage of OR nursing staff are in their 50s and 60s. Studies have revealed that OR staff have the second-lowest percentage of RNs who are under 40 (Association of periOperative Registered Nurses [AORN], 2015).

A primary driver for the OR nursing shortage has been the absence of OR content and clinical experiences in both associate and baccalaureate educational programs. Nursing students have minimal exposure to the content of OR nursing or hands-on clinical rotation. At best, some nursing students may get an opportunity to follow their assigned surgical patients into the OR as observers. Without this experience, and with limited exposure, graduating nurses lack an awareness of the opportunity to choose this clinical practice option (AORN, 2015).

A secondary driver for the OR nursing shortage is the investment healthcare organizations make in the development and maintenance of OR staff orientation programs. Full-time educators are required to develop the didactic, skills lab, specialty rotations, and preceptor training required. The basic orientation program takes from 6 to 9 months to develop a new staff member to a beginning level of performance. It takes another 1 to 2 years before the typical OR nurse gains a full base of experience across the multiple surgical specialties. Also, as more OR nurses retire, their experience and educational expertise exits the organization as well.

There is also an ongoing resistance to employ inexperienced OR nursing staff because of the flight risk these staff members may represent. It can be devastating to the department to lose a nurse after a significant investment of time and resources. It takes skillful interviewing of candidates to identify those who have both the professional and the technical aptitudes for success, in addition to the stamina and personal characteristics to survive in a high-pressure, complex environment.

MANAGEMENT OF OPERATING ROOM NURSING

OR nursing consists of two core roles: the RN who serves as a circulator in the OR (and who may also step into the scrub role), and the surgical technician (ST) who fulfills the scrub role most of the time.

The circulator is the member of the surgical team who has overall responsibility for the nursing care of the patient, safety of the patient and the environment, and all activities outside of the sterile field, while also monitoring the integrity of the sterile field. The scrub role assists the surgeon by preparing the sterile field, ensuring the availability of instrumentation and supplies needed for the case, and passing the instruments back and forth to the surgeon.

> *The Association of periOperative Registered Nurses (AORN) has developed clear standards for staffing mandating the presence of, at a minimum, one RN serving as a circulator for every OR case. Having a minimum of one experienced RN circulator dedicated to each patient undergoing an operative or other invasive procedure will provide for safe, quality patient care in the surgical arena (AORN, 2014).*

It is well known that the requirements for nurses' entry into practice have evolved from traditional hospital-based diploma programs to colleges and universities. Diploma-based programs had extensive clinical rotations that typically included the OR. This provided exposure and some measure of training for nurses in the program. Current academic programs have not included these educational opportunities given time and resource commitments, as well as the fact that most university curricula have simply become too full. Population and community health, and the myriad of evolving technologies and pharmaceuticals, consume a substantial share of educational experience. Also, keep in mind that inpatient utilization is declining in many markets; therefore, much of the assessment and technical component of education occurs in highly sophisticated simulation centers. The closest students in ADN or BSN programs get to the OR is through a brief observational experience with little or no background on the science or practice of OR nursing.

A similar transition has occurred for surgical technicians (STs). Prior to the 1970s, the majority of OR staff were STs in both scrub and circulator roles. These STs were trained on-the-job through hospital-based programs. Many came from a military background where they received extensive training and experience in the care of wounded soldiers. The hospital-based programs are now nonexistent; STs receive their basic training either from the military or, in growing numbers, through community college programs. Many hospitals have partnered with these community colleges to provide a site for hands-on clinical training. Indeed, this is an excellent source of recruitment for these valuable OR staff.

The greatest challenge healthcare leaders face lies in developing an ongoing stream of RNs and STs to meet the demands of surgical services' expanding case volume and replace staff that leave or retire. Meeting this demand is done by either recruiting experienced OR staff or training staff from within. The competition for recruiting experienced OR staff has risen sharply because this highly specialized workforce is shrinking.

Addressing Recruitment Challenges

Many human resources (HR) departments are reacting to overall nursing recruitment challenges by creating competitive salary, compensation, and bonus programs to attract experienced staff. Typically, the salary ranges for RNs and STs do not vary across clinical specialties, including surgical services. In some markets this may limit the ability to offer higher starting rates for experienced OR staff. It is the unique HR department that considers focused recruitment strategies and tactics for the OR. Successful recruitment of experienced OR nursing staff may warrant extraordinary measures and creative strategies to reduce long-term vacancy rates.

There is some measure of debate on the benefit of recruiting new graduates to the OR. Some leaders feel new graduates need some time on an inpatient nursing unit to hone their basic nursing knowledge, assessment, and relationship skills before being able to function effectively as an OR nurse. The risks related to the care of the surgical patient require a sense of confidence and the judgement and communication skills to truly collaborate as a member of an interdisciplinary team.

Others feel this general unit experience is not necessary if the OR training program is designed to accommodate new graduates. No definitive studies have been conducted to support the need for new graduates to work on an inpatient unit prior to joining the OR staff (Anderson, Fricke, Gunn, Sochacki, & Nolan, 1975).

Even with the best recruitment programs, most healthcare organizations cannot rely solely on recruitment of experienced OR staff and, therefore, need to develop their own OR training programs. In doing so, their options are either to develop a hospital-based program de novo or to purchase a fully developed program that can be customized to the hospital's individual needs and culture.

The most popular program is AORN's Periop101: A Core Curriculum OR (Periop 101 A Core Curriculum). This program is a comprehensive didactic, laboratory skill, and preceptor-based program designed to provide basic knowledge and training in a variety of specialties for OR nurses. An annual fee, based on number of students, is paid for access to the program and all materials. Some (but not many) colleges also have established an elective experience in the OR or provide continuing education programs using AORN's curriculum. Hospitals may find it beneficial to partner with these schools in training staff, while reciprocally providing access to their ORs for clinical experiential training.

The basic OR orientation and training program includes rotations through each of the surgical specialties to expose new staff to the nuances of each specialty. The objective is to provide the basic knowledge and skill required for each specialty so that the new OR staff member can develop basic competencies to meet the needs of cases that require staffing while on call. The length of these surgical specialty rotations can be anywhere from 6 to 12 months. There may be conflict in designing programs that can move new OR staff through the program as efficiently as possible while also ensuring the development of basic competency levels required for nurses to be safe and productive members of the OR staff.

Once a new OR staff member completes a basic program, a deliberate and thoughtful experiential assignment rotation should be established.

Best practice suggests that 1 year of rotation through the variety of surgical specialties is required to ensure deeper competencies and confidence. These staff members can gain the experience required to plan patient care with surgeons and anesthesia staff while ensuring the highest quality and efficient performance of surgical cases.

Recognizing Advanced Competencies Through Certification Programs

The Association of Surgical Technologists (AST) and the Association of periOperative Nurses (AORN) have established external clinical certification programs to support the ongoing development and recognition of highly experienced staff. These certifications are encouraged by many healthcare organizations through salary stipends and other awards for achievement. There is a growing trend in some states requiring certification for at least the ST workforce. In an organization pursuing Magnet status, specialty certification of staff is highly encouraged. Magnet recognition, provided through the American Nurses Credentialing Center (ANCC), is the highest level of recognition for nursing excellence.

Operating Room Nurse Practice Specialization

Another area of ongoing debate in managing surgical services is around the concept of specialization. Historically, OR staff were expected to maintain competencies to perform any case, at any time. One day they might be assigned to general surgery cases and the next to orthopedics.

However, levels of clinical and technical knowledge have advanced rapidly as more complex surgical interventions are required for performing surgical procedures. It has become nearly impossible to maintain the knowledge, and attain high competency levels, to scrub and circulate for all surgical specialties. This is especially true in hospitals with a mix of inpatient and complex outpatient cases. Given technological advances, what were once considered "simple" inpatient cases have been moved to outpatient and ambulatory surgery center facilities, with even more complex total joint and spinal surgery cases being performed in ambulatory surgery centers as well.

Surgeons will often complain about a lack of experienced staff within the OR setting. They experience inconsistent levels of staff performance when they do not work with the same staff on a consistent basis. Their cases may be delayed due to incomplete preparation of supplies, instruments, or equipment. Surgical procedure time may be extended because OR staff are not familiar with the sequencing steps and options for certain procedures. Surgeons are increasingly demanding surgical specialty teams, composed of consistent staff members who plan closely with surgeons and anesthesia and manage the ever-growing and highly specialized technology required for patient care delivery.

The extent of OR staff specialization has been developing for many years. It can be seen informally in assignment patterns whereby certain staff are frequently assigned to specific rooms or cases, or it may be formalized through a team structure with leaders assigned specific responsibilities for patient care planning and supply, instrument or equipment management. These teams are referred to as *specialty teams, pods,* or *cluster staffing.* They allow staff to concentrate their training, provide consistent patient care, and develop in-depth knowledge and skills for specific specialties or types of cases within a specialty (Biala, 2008).

Surgical services management needs to address these needs with a consistent and comprehensive surgical specialty team program that meets staff needs and provides the same standard of care for all specialties. Developing specialization in the context of a formal nurse practice model provides a structure for successful management and shared governance. The design, organization, and ongoing development of the specialty team model should be led by the OR staff themselves, with appropriate direction from surgical services management. This unit-based taskforce, or ongoing nurse practice committee, should be provided with information on the strategic growth of surgical specialties, the need for experienced and competent staff, and input on improvement needed from surgeons and staff.

The OR specialization group should research the various models for specialization and confirm the extent or degree of specialization for staff to maintain. This is often accomplished by picking a spot along the OR staff specialization continuum.

SPECIALIZATION AS A CONTINUUM

Specialization can be thought of as a continuum of OR nursing practice.

Generalist	Generalist with Specialist Preferences	Specialist with Generalist Competencies	Specialist/ Subspecialist

Figure 6.1 Specialization as a Continuum

A *generalist practice model,* on one end of the continuum, sets an expectation that all nurses and technicians will maintain competencies across all specialties. Under this practice model, staff are completely trained and maintain competency for all specialties. Few ORs are successfully maintaining this model, and if they are, only in very small departments.

On the other end of the continuum lies the *specialist/subspecialist model* in which nurses and technicians are assigned to a single specialty and may even subspecialize in certain types of cases, equipment, or patient interventions. Staff only work within their specialty and are not expected to provide patient care outside of their specialty. Often, these teams provide on-call staff 24 hours a day, 7 days a week. Most departments will find themselves somewhere in between these two models.

The *generalist with specialist preferences model* is an informal model where staff are assigned more consistently to one–three specialties, but also are expected to be prepared to do most cases within every specialty. This allows for some measure of beginning specialization as experience is gained.

The *specialist with generalist competencies* model formally identifies staff that have specialized on one–three specialties and are routinely assigned to just these cases. They are, however, expected to maintain general competencies for specific cases, equipment, or patient interventions for other specialties. These general competencies reflect the type of patients who would present themselves in on-call situations.

It is important to note that staff with a general competency have a solid perioperative nursing knowledge base. Staff members are required to complete orientation and basic rotation across specialties. The rotation, however, is focused on exposure and achieving competency for the specific cases, equipment, and patient interventions that all staff would need for serving in an on-call status. Often this same type of preparation supports daily assignments when there is not enough case volume within a specific specialty.

Deciding where a department should fall on the continuum is most often driven by case volume and complexity. Staff satisfaction and commitment to the degree of specialization in their practices are also crucial considerations. Identifying and managing the best nurse practice model for the department requires a step-by-step methodology to review options and ensure a successful transition (Biala, 2008).

Operating Room Nursing Budget

Challenges related to the appropriate number of OR staff FTEs are endless. Many finance departments apply an approach (also used in other inpatient care units) whereby a ratio of worked hours is calculated based on a workload measure. For ORs, this generally reflects the number of surgical cases or case minutes.

Using case minutes to determine staffing needs is by far the better measure because it more closely reflects when OR staff are engaged in patient care. This is the same approach that is taken in national comparative databases. The problem with this measure, however, is that it typically does not reflect acuity or the different levels of staff that may be required for a case. For instance, some intricate or difficult cases may legitimately require a second scrub or circulator.

These high-level ratios should be considered as directional and validated based on the staffing plan for the rooms and hours open for surgeon case scheduling. More recently this has been referred to as OR resource hours. Resource hours are determined based on the organization's scheduling and block distribution plan (see Chapter 4) and utilized in planning.

Once FTE requirements are confirmed, a decision needs to be made on the appropriate balance of RNs to ST staff. This decision is often made based on national targets, adjusted as necessary based on the regional supply of surgical technicians and the ability to recruit.

CONSIDERATIONS IN MANAGEMENT OF PERIANESTHESIA NURSING

Perianesthesia nursing is a more recent term that applies to nursing staff caring for patients from the moment the surgical case is scheduled, throughout preoperative preparation and postoperative care. These staff members are sometimes referred to as preadmission testing/care (PAT/PAC), pre-op staff, post-anesthesia care unit (PACU), or recovery room and post-op staff.

When the OR becomes the focus of care, referred to as being "OR-centric," these patient care units may be overlooked or treated as second-class in the world of surgical services. However, the proper management of the patient before and after the surgical procedure has an equally significant impact on surgical outcomes (Franklin & Franklin, 2017).

Healthcare executives may hear frequent complaints of "back-ups" in PACU when inpatient beds are unavailable. Hospital bed management processes can be very challenging. The timing of patient discharges, bed turnover processes, and pressing needs to relieve high census in the emergency department are important components of demand that must be focused on throughout the day. These demands often result in a hold on discharges from the PACU. These holds may fill the recovery bays and create back-ups in the OR because patients cannot be transported out of the OR and into PACU. This phenomenon creates a great deal of stress within surgical services and stresses staffing across the area.

Staff also complain when patient delays result because the preoperative unit did not get the patient ready in time for the OR. While close co-ordination of pre-op care is the key to avoiding these occurrences, other dynamics may actually impact the root cause. Decisions made in the

OR regarding scheduling and sequencing of cases, plus changes to the schedule throughout the day, will have a direct impact on the timing, flow of patients, and staffing on these units (Sandberg et al., 2005).

Recruitment, training, and development of perianesthesia staff are additional considerations for the surgical services management team. Nursing staff assigned to recovery require very specific competencies. Excellent programs have been developed and maintained by the American Society for PeriAnesthesia Nurses (ASPAN). Critical care certifications are requirements for recovery staff and should minimally include ASCLS and PALS. In addition, highly specific certifications for recovery nurses should be encouraged, typically CPAN and CAPA. The American Society of Anesthesiologists (ASA) works very closely with ASPAN in developing standards of care and professional performance.

Preadmission testing units provide preoperative patient care and are often the location where surgical patients arrive on the day of surgery. In this area, nursing, anesthesia staff, and surgeons conduct preoperative patient assessments. Surgical services postoperative care occurs in the post-anesthesia care unit (PACU), once known as the recovery room. This is where primary, or Phase 1, anesthesia recovery occurs. Inpatients are eventually discharged to an inpatient care unit while outpatients are typically transferred to a Phase 2 recovery unit. Here they receive extended observation and final education before discharge from the hospital.

An emerging trend in the construction of new facilities is the consolidation of preoperative and postoperative care for all procedure care departments. This stems from the recognition that patient care processes and basic nursing competencies are nearly identical for pre- and post-care for ORs and procedural or interventional units. If this universal center is geographically located near the procedure units, then cardiac, radiology, and endoscopy patients can be transported back and forth. This consolidation results in decreased costs and higher staff productivity. Nursing staff on these units maintain a similar set of basic competencies; subsets of staff may develop deeper specialization for recovering the more complex procedures in a similar manner to OR specialty teams.

Greater attention is now being focused on the management of these units and their effect on efficiencies, quality outcomes, and cost. Following is a review of best practices in the management of processes and resources for each unit (Franklin & Franklin, 2017).

Managing Preadmission Testing

Preadmission patient preparation and testing (PAT) has become a vital part of the surgical patient care continuum. Establishing a well-functioning nursing team with strong anesthesia alignment is key to implementing best practices and achieving high-quality outcomes. Following is a list of the key elements, or best practices, for managing PAT.

- All (100%) electively scheduled patients should be assessed, prepared, and contacted before the scheduled day of surgery.

- PAT nursing staff should start the PAT process as soon as possible after the patient is scheduled. A patient chart should be initiated, and the process begins.

- PAT staff should contact the patient to conduct a phone screening and nursing assessment to confirm the extent of preoperative preparation required. A standardized patient care algorithm can be established, with anesthesia and surgeon input that identifies the preparation care pathway and required tests based on the procedure and patient age, health, and comorbidities.

- The following list of key elements also need to be managed:

  - Preregistration and insurance verification

  - Nursing preoperative assessment

  - Surgeon and anesthesia preoperative orders

  - Ordering and completion of required preoperative lab tests, EKGs, and X-rays where applicable

  - Ensuring that any preoperative consults are complete

  - Obtaining a patient history and physical

  - Obtaining the operative patient consent

  - Providing preoperative patient education and basic information such as special diet and medication instructions, as well as arrival times and directions

  - Anesthesia review and assessment of select patients with higher risk for anesthesia

A hand-off of this patient information then occurs between the PAT and preoperative staff. Patient readiness often is covered during the caseload management huddle the day before surgery to identify and resolve any incomplete prep or abnormal test results.

Managing Preoperative Care

The day of surgery for patients and their families is stressful and needs to be managed through evidence-based care processes. First impressions are formed as the patient checks in at admitting and registration. Subsequent interactions with staff are key to relieving anxiety and achieving high levels of patient satisfaction.

The vast majority of both outpatients and inpatients arrive the day of surgery. Specific plans of care need to be established to meet the variable care demands of different patients and procedures. Several healthcare providers will need to evaluate the patient's readiness for surgery during the short period of time they are on the preoperative care unit.

Best practices for managing preoperative care include:

- Admitting and registration should identify and process surgical patients with a higher priority to ensure they will arrive on the preoperative unit quickly to prevent delays. Some organizations have moved admitting and registration for surgical patients to the preoperative unit.

- Close supervision of patient flow, placement of patients to patient care bays, and staff assignment are required due to shifting minute-by-minute dynamics on the preoperative care unit and the OR.

- Frequent communication should occur with the OR control desk and OR coordinators on changes to the surgical schedule. Many organizations are physically combining the OR and preoperative unit control desks. Many departments also are now using patient flow monitors that report patient status to augment verbal communication.

- Preoperative nursing admission is a protected time for the preoperative staff to admit the patient, conduct nursing assessment, and complete any last-minute tests as ordered. Anesthesia, surgeons and OR staff should then follow with their evaluations and interactions with the patient. These activities should be carefully planned and orchestrated. A typical workflow coordinating these activities is provided in the T-Minus table (Figure 6.2).

T-Minus 120	T-Minus 90	T-Minus 35	T-Minus 30	T-Minus 15	T-Minus 10	T-Minus 5	Scheduled Case Start	T-Plus 1
0530-0545	0600-0655	0700-0710 0655 PNB*	0700-0715	0715 0705 PNB*	0720	0725	0730	0731
Surgical patient arrives at registration.	Surgical patient arrives in pre-op. Chart processing is completed (H&P, consent, nursing pre-op phone assessment, lab/test results, insurance pre-authorization). All orders are reviewed (anesthesia/surgeon/ proceduralist orders).	All pre-op nursing activities are completed. PNB* patients are moved to PACU by 0655. If patient not moved to PACU, anesthesia or surgeon may see patient on day of Surgery.	All anesthesia activities are completed (unless series of OR cases does not allow anesthesiologist to perform pre-op assessment until immediately prior to OR start time).	Surgeon, surgical resident/fellow, proceduralist, or proceduralist resident/fellow identify the patient, verify the procedure and surgical site, and initial the site in a location that will be visible when draped.	OR nurse completes assessment of patient before 0720.	All periop activities on the surgical checklist are verified and signed by OR nurse prior to patient transport.	Patient in room.	First case of the day is considered late.

Subsequent cases are at risk of being late. |

* PNB = Peripheral Nerve Block patients

Figure 6.2 SHC Sample T-Minus Table

Used with permission from Sullivan Healthcare Consulting

A handoff of this patient information then occurs between the perioperative staff and the staff member who will transport the patient to the
OR.

Managing PACU (or Phase 1 and Phase 2 Recovery)

Most surgical patients need close monitoring as they emerge and recover from anesthesia. The first 15 minutes are critical and require at
least a one-to-one nurse to patient ratio. As with preoperative care,
specific plans of care need to be established to meet the variable care
demands of different patients and procedures. A comprehensive hand-
off needs to occur between anesthesia and the OR nurse to ensure vital
patient condition information is passed on that might alter the standard plan of care.

Following is a list of the key elements, or best practices, for managing
patient recovery.

- Similarly to the preoperative care unit, close supervision of patient flow, placement of patients to patient care bays, and staff
  assignments is required because of shifting minute-by-minute
  dynamics on the postoperative care unit and in the OR. In addition, recovery staff supervision needs to include the status of
  inpatient beds to manage any potential back-ups or holds on
  the recovery unit.

- PACU managers should directly participate in hospital-wide
  bed management planning and daily management activities.

- With anesthesia, establish clear Phase 1 discharge criteria,
  based on patient recovery parameters.

- Identify patients who can bypass the Phase 1 recovery experience, based on the type of case and anesthesia used. This is often referred to as "fast tracking" the patient.

■ With anesthesia and surgeons, establish clear Phase 2 discharge criteria, based on patient recovery parameters. Specific surgical postoperative and discharge instructions should be developed and given to the patient.

Perianesthesia Nursing Budget

Several organizations have begun consolidating preoperative and post-operative nurse staffing budgets to improve productivity. These units experience wide variations in patient occupancy throughout the day. Variation of 3 to 12 total patients may occur on a 12-bay unit through-out the day. This variation has been partially addressed by expanding traditional shifts to more closely match patient demand (e.g., 6:00–2:30, 8:00–4:30, and 10:00–6:30, etc.).

While adding additional shifts has helped raise productivity for indi-vidual units, mapping concurrent patient demand for several units has revealed an opportunity to move staff between units to maximize pro-ductivity. Cross-training staff, and cross coverage to these units, has also seen some measures of success. Not all staff need to be cross-trained to achieve productivity increases; this is good because not all staff will be interested in cross-training. (See Figure 6.3).

Creating a Healthy Environment

Not only is the notion of creating a healthy perioperative environment supported by a number of professional organizations—including the American College of Surgeons, Association of periOperative Regis-tered Nurses (AORN), American Society of Anesthesiologists, Ameri-can Nurses Association, and American Association of Critical-Care Nurses—but there is a growing body of evidence supporting the fact that a collegial practice environment with open communication leads to improved clinical outcomes and greatly satisfied staff. AORN (2015) has developed a position statement that clearly articulates the need for leaders to facilitate the creation of a highly functioning perioperative team predicated on the ability to communicate, collaborate, and respect each other's roles and skill sets.

UCC - Jun-Aug-Sep							
	Total	Average	Minimum	Maximum		Average +	Staff
	Number	Number	Number	Number	Standard	1 Standard	Ratio
Hour of Day	Patients	Patients	Patients	Patients	Deviation	Deviation	
0:00-1:00	0	0.00	0	0	0.00	0.00	0.00
1:00-2:00	0	0.00	0	0	0.00	0.00	0.00
2:00-3:00	0	0.00	0	0	0.00	0.00	0.00
3:00-4:00	0	0.00	0	0	0.00	0.00	0.00
4:00-5:00	0	0.00	0	0	0.00	0.00	0.00
5:00-6:00	4	0.07	0	1	0.25	0.32	0.18
6:00-7:00	378	6.30	0	10	2.22	8.52	4.14
7:00-8:00	790	13.17	4	19	3.48	16.65	7.86
8:00-9:00	930	15.50	8	23	3.57	19.07	8.84
9:00-10:00	1059	17.65	11	26	3.67	21.32	9.56
10:00-11:00	1076	17.93	10	28	3.37	21.30	9.56
11:00-12:00	1065	17.75	8	28	3.96	21.71	9.56
12:00-13:00	1002	16.70	8	27	3.94	20.64	9.02
13:00-14:00	826	13.77	6	21	3.62	17.39	7.76
14:00-15:00	564	9.40	3	16	3.09	12.49	5.48
15:00-16:00	337	5.62	1	14	3.04	8.65	3.86
16:00-17:00	184	3.07	0	9	2.15	5.22	2.31
17:00-18:00	124	2.07	0	8	1.83	3.90	1.60
18:00-19:00	72	1.20	0	5	1.30	2.50	1.00
19:00-20:00	36	0.60	0	4	0.89	1.49	0.55
20:00-21:00	0	0.00	0	0	0.00	0.00	0.00
21:00-22:00	0	0.00	0	0	0.00	0.00	0.00
22:00-23:00	0	0.00	0	0	0.00	0.00	0.00
23:00-24:00	0	0.00	0	0	0.00	0.00	0.00
					Staff Hours:		81
Note: Data represents three months (June/Aug/Sept 2017)					Min. # Staff Per Day:		10.84
Staff ratio calculated using average + one standard deviation					Benefit Time (15%):		1.63
ASPAN guideline: minimum PACU staffing of 2							
Staff hours=7.5 hrs per day					**Total FTEs Recommended:**		**12.46**

Manojlovich and DeCicco (2007), in their study of 25 critical care units, assessed the effectiveness of nurse-physician communication and found a significant correlation between communication and patient safety outcomes. Nurok, Sundt, and Frankel (2011) suggest that there is a growing body of literature demonstrating a relationship between teamwork and communication in the perioperative environment and discrete, measurable, clinically relevant outcomes.

| | | Actual | | | Actual | Variance |
| | | Preop/Postop/UCC | | | Total | Actual vs Model |
Charge RN	RN Preop	GI	Phase II	PCT		
					-	-
					-	-
					-	-
					-	-
					-	-
0.13				0.50	0.63	0.44
0.50	5.00	1.00		2.25	8.75	4.61
0.50	5.00	2.50	0.25	4.00	12.25	4.39
0.50	5.00	4.00	1.00	5.00	15.50	6.66
0.50	5.00	4.00	2.50	5.00	17.00	7.44
0.50	5.00	4.00	3.50	5.00	18.00	8.44
0.50	5.00	4.00	4.00	5.00	18.50	8.94
0.50	5.00	4.00	4.00	3.50	17.00	7.98
0.13	2.50	4.00	4.00	3.00	13.63	5.87
		2.00	4.00	2.75	8.75	3.27
		0.50	3.25	1.50	5.25	1.39
			2.50	1.00	3.50	1.19
			1.00	1.00	2.00	0.40
				1.00	1.00	0.00
				1.00	1.00	0.45
				1.00	1.00	1.00
				1.00	1.00	1.00
				0.50	0.50	0.50
					-	-
			Staff Hours:		145	63.97
			Min. # Staff Per Day		19.37	8.53
			Benefit Time (15%):		2.91	1.28
			Total FTEs:		**22.27**	**9.81**

Figure 6.3   SHC Sample Cross Coverage Multiple Units

Used with permission from Sullivan Healthcare Consulting

EXECUTIVE LEADERSHIP LESSONS

- It is becoming increasingly difficult to recruit and retain experienced surgical (OR) nurses. This is at a time when surgical procedures are becoming more complex and technology-dependent. Because of increasing clinical risk and surgeon recognition of the importance of an experienced staff to clinical outcomes, surgeons are increasingly requesting a consistent team.

- Demographic workforce data suggests that the average age of an OR nurse is significantly higher than the general nursing population. Therefore, ORs across the country are facing a number of retirements of experienced staff.

- Inexperienced staff orientation programs are very costly, lengthy, and resource-intensive. In financial terms, these human resources are considered nonproductive for 6 to 12 months (not included in staffing), yet the organization is making a sizable investment in their training.

- There is significant debate among OR leaders regarding the benefit of hiring new graduate nurses directly to the OR versus after some time on an inpatient unit. The time on the unit may help hone assessment skills and build the confidence required to be an active participant of the surgical team. However, there is little empirical evidence to suggest one option is more favorable for either nurse engagement or clinical outcomes.

- For those organizations without the means to develop and direct their own OR orientation program, purchasing the AORN curriculum or partnering with local colleges may be viable alternatives. As more organizations become part of a larger system, a system-based training program is often cost effective.

- Once upon a time, OR nurses were expected to be able to perform competently in all types of cases and all specialties. The rapid proliferation of technology, the increasing difficulty and sophistication of the types of procedures, as well as the comorbidities experienced by many surgical patients, have made the notion of a generalist OR nurse nearly obsolete.

- Specialized staffing facilitates the participation of nurses in the interdisciplinary planning of care, improvement of systems and processes, and purchase of equipment. It also leads to improved staff and physician engagement.

- Using case minutes to determine staffing needs is by far the best measure for determining the staffing budget. This is the same approach that is taken in national comparative databases, allowing the ability to benchmark productivity and budget data. The problem with this measure, however, is that it typically does not reflect acuity or the different levels of staff that may be required for a case. For instance, some intricate or difficult cases may legitimately require a second scrub or circulator.

- Perianesthesia nursing is a more recent term that applies to nursing staff who care for patients from the moment the surgical case is scheduled, throughout preoperative preparation and postoperative care. These staff are sometimes referred to as preadmission testing/care (PAT/PAC), pre-op staff, postoperative care unit (PACU) or recovery room and post-op staff. Clinical outcomes are much improved when the patient's care is approached holistically and managed across clinical silos.

- There is an emerging trend to consolidate all surgical, interventional, and procedural pre- and postoperative/procedure care in a single location. Staff have identical competency requirements; therefore, presuming it is geographically possible, there are many staff productivity benefits of this arrangement.

REFERENCES

Anderson, S., Fricke, E., Gunn, L., Sochacki, C., & Nolan, M. G. (1975). The new raduate in the operating room. *Nursing Clinics of North America, 10*(4), 655–665.

AORN Position Statement on a healthy perioperative practice environment. (2015). AORN, Inc. Retrieved from https://www.aorn.org/-/media/aorn/guidelines/position-statements/posstat-safety-healthy-practice.pdf

Association of periOperative Registered Nurses (AORN). (2014, March). *AORN position statement on perioperative safe staffing and on-call practices.* Retrieved from https://www.aorn.org/-/media/aorn/guidelines/position-statements/posstat-personnel-safe-staffing-on-call-practices.pdf

Association of periOperative Registered Nurses (AORN). (2015, November). *Perioperative succession planning: Theoretical learning, clinical opportunities, and residencies.* AORN Transition to Practice Ad Hoc Committee. Retrieved from https://www.aorn.org/-/media/aorn/guidelines/position-statements/14783-whitepaper-v6.pdf

Biala, G. (2008, August). Specialty staff versus generalists: How do ORs strike the balance? *OR Manager, 24*(8). Retrieved from https://www.ormanager.com

Franklin, J., & Franklin, T. (2017). Improving preoperative throughput. *Journal of PeriAnesthesia Nursing, 32*(1), 38–44. doi: 10.1016/j.jopan.2015.03.012

Manojlovich, M., & DeCicco, B. (2007). Healthy work environments, nurse-physician communication, and patient outcomes. *American Journal of Critical Care, 16*(6), 536–543.

Nurok, M., Sundt, T. M., & Frankel, A. (2011). Teamwork and communication in the operating room: Relationship to discrete outcomes and research challenges. *Anesthesiology Clinics, 29,* 1–11.

Patterson, P. (2012, December). Who will replace retiring perioperative nurses? *OR Manager, 28*(12). Retrieved from https://www.ormanager.com

Sandberg, W., Daily, B., Egan, M., Stahl, J. E., Goldman, J. M., Wiklund, R. A., & Rattner, D. (2005). Deliberate perioperative systems design improves operating room throughput. *Anesthesiology, 103*(2), 406–418.

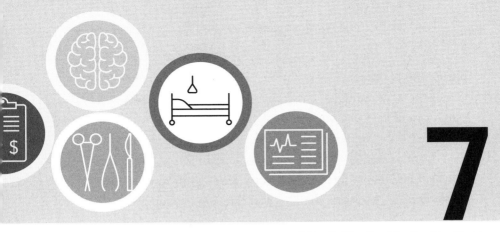

7

PHYSICIAN SERVICES

Surgical service leaders often feel that complaints from surgeons and anesthesiologists never seem to end. Surgical services is a high-risk, high-stress environment where the alignment of priorities between providers and administrative leaders is becoming increasingly difficult. Scheduling issues, process inefficiencies, delays, and availability of trained staff—along with supply, instrumentation, and equipment accessibility—are just some of the variables that add to the complexity of meeting physician needs. A seasoned colleague once said that he "never met a surgeon who was completely satisfied." Although there may be some truth in this, many organizations are finding ways to work effectively with their physicians, providing evidence that creating successful partnerships is possible.

History demonstrates significant levels of dissatisfaction between healthcare administrators and physicians. National healthcare policies and local administrative responses to these policies have negatively affected the profitability of many physician practices. Increasing documentation requirements, declines in procedure reimbursement, productivity standards for employed physicians, malpractice implications, and competitive pressures are a few of the environmental challenges confronting both hospitals and physicians alike. On a positive note, however, turmoil often provides the impetus for innovation and heretofore-unseen collaboration. With the advent of shared decision-making, access to data, and a desire for transparency, many organizations have seen significant productivity improvements, increases in surgical volume, more engaged staff and physicians—and in turn, heralded improvements to clinical outcomes.

Although these dynamics may exacerbate high levels of dissatisfaction between physicians and healthcare administrators, these same market dynamics are requiring them to work more closely to survive and thrive. Medical literature abounds with publications on the best strategies and tactics to improve relationships through stronger physician alignment models. Strengthening hospital-physician alignment is a top priority for executives (Clark, 2013). There are a wide variety of models that organizations are deploying to improve alignment, including various partnerships structures with both private and group practices, entering into employment relationships with physicians, and comanagement arrangements to name a few.

The surgical services administrator needs to be aware of physician alignment strategies and models and apply this knowledge in engaging with physicians in managing patient care administration. Engaging surgeons and anesthesiologists has some unique challenges. Years of education and clinical training have obviously been focused on developing diagnostic and technical expertise as well as the confidence to practice autonomously. Physician practice emphasizes clinical problem-solving and implementing decisions in immediate or short timeframes (Merlino, 2015). Few physicians have received, or even been exposed to, training in management processes. This has led to frustration on the part of the physician who simply wants the best care for the patient with as little fuss as possible in the surgical setting. The good news, however, is that the management process closely resembles the clinical diagnostic and treatment process.

In addition to this management-training gap, surgical services have confused the hospital-physician relationship by historically labeling patients as customers. The term "customer" connotes someone purchasing a product or service and does not reflect the true patient-provider partnership model required today. Physicians should always be respected for the clinical knowledge and experience they have gained over years of education and practice. They are the clinical practice leaders assuming the highest risks in rendering high quality and safe patient care. This role and responsibility needs to be consistently recognized in partnering with physicians to improve processes, systems, and outcomes.

Thoughtful and consistent communication is key to getting started with physicians in surgical services. This includes:

- Gaining an understanding of their practices and identifying their key goals.

- Meeting with them to confirm a sincere desire to work together.

- Discussing the organization's challenges and goals and identifying the overlap that will inevitably be noted.

- Fixing operational issues. For many, this will positively impact their productivity and ability to perform more surgical cases.

- Helping them understand the business, recognizing the critical need for their involvement, and promising to deliver.

Partnering in this way helps foster mutual goal-setting and the activities and steps required to achieve those goals. Transparency, mutual agreements on priorities, setting realistic timelines—and then delivering—will be the keys to success.

WORKING IN TANDEM WITH ANESTHESIA SERVICES

The surgical services executive can expect to hear frequent complaints about anesthesia services, most frequently around the availability of an anesthesia services provider when needed, or when delays occur. Care needs to be taken to fully understand the complaint and to determine its root cause, coverage, performance, or contract-related issues. Inevitably, various system and process misalignments will be identified when investigating anesthesia delays. Through understanding the root cause and withholding blame, the surgical services administrator will learn that anesthesia leaders can be their best allies in solving surgical services performance issues.

The majority of organizations continue to work with the same anesthesia practice group for years. Often contracts are renewed with few, if any, modifications to reflect the changing dynamics of managing surgical services. The best practice for contract review is to conduct meetings with group leaders to discuss what needs to be covered in the contract and gain consensus before engaging legal support.

Occasionally, anesthesia services may be deemed unacceptable, and the need to look at alternative options is warranted. It is better to do this after meeting with the current practice leaders to resolve any differences. The goal should be to establish clear expectations and memorialize them in the contracting process.

Critical anesthesia contract components that should be considered are:

- The coverage plan for OR and non-OR sites (e.g., obstetrics and endoscopy)
- Medical leadership
- Performance expectations, metrics, and frequency for monitoring
- Financial support

Anesthesia Coverage Plan

An anesthesia services coverage plan should reflect OR resource hours contained in the surgical services scheduling guidelines (see Chapter 5, "Performance Management"). These guidelines identify the number of OR suites or procedure rooms that are open and staffed to meet surgeon case schedule demand. They may vary by day and by hour during the course of the day. Coverage for nonelective cases and on-call demand are addressed in the overall anesthesia coverage plan. For example, obstetric coverage is always defined both for routine and for urgent or emergent C-sections and deliveries. There also should be a clear process defined for when and how the coverage plan will be changed within the term of the contract.

Typically, elective resource hours are staffed either with an anesthesiologist or with a certified registered nurse anesthetist (CRNA) under the supervision of an anesthesiologist. Exceptions are present in those states that allow for a CRNA to administer anesthesia under the supervision of the surgeon. This anesthesia practice model is determined by the medical staff based on complexities of patient care specific to the organization. The practice model chosen also is dependent on the market availability of anesthesiologists and CRNAs. Regional differences will affect the balance of the anesthesia practice model.

The question of employing CRNAs also may be considered by an organization. The literature does not point to a single best practice related to the employment or contracting of CRNAs or whether employment by the anesthesia group or hospital is more favorable. There have been no clear benefits established other than an experiential wisdom that it is better to consolidate anesthesia services into one corporate umbrella to avoid duplication of management processes.

In addition, anesthesia services coverage has grown substantially to encompass several sites outside of OR suites. *Non-OR anesthesia* (NORA) refers to administration of sedation/anesthesia outside the OR for patients undergoing painful or uncomfortable procedures (Metzner & Domino, 2010). Some examples of these areas include endoscopy, radiology, cardiology, and pain management for inpatients. Procedure demand in these areas may not be consistent or prescheduled, requiring that anesthesia plan extra staff who may not be engaged in patient care, creating poor productivity.

The alternative is to assign one out-of-OR anesthesia provider who covers all areas. This may cause delays if one area must wait for the anesthesia provider to be finished in another area. The solution is to ensure the NORA sites are clearly identified with expectations in coverage provided by day of week and hour of day. This coverage should denote if it is by a dedicated anesthesia provider or shared across a group of NORA sites.

Anesthesia Department Medical Leadership

Key leadership roles and responsibilities need to be defined in the anesthesia contract, along with any compensation to be paid to the anesthesia group for these activities. Typically the roles include an anesthesia department chairperson or chief, anesthesia medical director, and chief CRNA. The requirement and responsibilities for the department chair or chief are found in the medical staff organization's bylaws. These usually address responsibilities for clinical oversight of anesthesia patient care delivery and clinical oversights for preadmission testing, preoperative and postoperative care.

The anesthesia medical director is a newer role that helps the hospital manage all surgical services resources. Experience has shown this role is typically filled by a dedicated anesthesiologist who spends a minimum of 30% of the time in these management duties. This individual should not be counted when staffing rooms. These responsibilities are covered in more detail in Chapter 2, "Governance and Managing Resources." In some organizations, these two roles may be combined into one. Lastly, a portion of salary may be reimbursed for a chief CRNA who manages CRNA coverage and assignments. This most often occurs in large, multisite surgical services departments.

In addition to defining roles and responsibilities, the contract should identify the mutual selection and evaluation processes. The organization should be included in succession planning and recruitment. Specific timeframes, such as quarterly reviews, should be scheduled for performance reviews. This ensures the organization's direct input in managing these roles.

Anesthesia Performance Expectations

Performance expectations are most often managed in tandem with overall surgical services performance management. Many key performance indicators overlap, such as first case on-time starts, OR suite turnover, and overall room utilization (see Chapter 5). There are, however, a few additional anesthesia-specific measures that should be considered in the anesthesia contract:

- Patient medical records to be reviewed by anesthesia the day before surgery for final sign-off

- Preanesthesia activities to be completed at least 15 minutes before scheduled in-room time

- Penalties for closing a site of coverage strictly for anesthesia staffing reasons

- Consistencies between anesthesia providers

- Anesthesia-related complications

As with medical leadership reviews, specific timeframes such as quarterly reviews should be scheduled for performance expectation reviews. More recently, portions of a subsidy are placed in an at-risk category based on the anesthesia group meeting targets of performance. Figure 7.1 displays a set of representative incentives to be considered in anesthesia contracts.

	All electively scheduled surgery patients to have a complete and reviewed chart by 1:00 p.m. the business day before
Percentage of Patients Evaluated Preadmission	scheduled surgery.
First Case On-Time Starts	95%
Patient Satisfaction	95%
Surgeon Satisfaction	95%
Unilaterally Closing a Room	Never
Total	

Financial Support

Subsidies, which may be included in the anesthesia services contract, are a growing concern for healthcare executives. These also are known as "stipends." Surveys by The Medical Group Management Association (MGMA) estimate that 85% of all hospitals subsidize the anesthesia groups in some way. The typical range is $100,000–$150,000 per anesthetizing location, per year (MGMA, n.d.) These subsidies are paid when the anesthesia practice's billing and collections are insufficient to maintain an economically viable practice. This most often occurs in hospitals requiring full-time coverage in areas with low billable patient volume such as obstetrics, or in organizations with high case mixes of Medicaid or similar low-paying payers.

The methods for establishing the subsidy are variable. The most common is based on a utilization model where a portion of the subsidy is paid when anesthesia coverage sites have a utilization or billable volume of below 70%. This model provides a clear methodology for subsidizing the practice income. It also provides an economic incentive to raise utilization levels at each site to achieve the highest levels of productivity. This is most often evident in the theory of vertical- versus horizontal-case scheduling.

75% to 85%	85% to 95%	95% TO 100%	$150,500
85% TO 90%	90% TO 95%	95% TO 100%	$150,500
75% to 80%	80% to 90%	90% to 100%	$205,750
75% to 80%	80% to 90%	90% to 100%	$205,750
Less often than 10%	Less often than 5%	Less often than 1%	$250,000
			$1.1 Million

FIGURE 7.1   SHC Physician Services

Anesthesia has always been a strong advocate of *vertical scheduling*, in which an operating or procedure room is completely filled before other rooms are opened. In theory, this drives the highest levels of utilization. On the contrary, *horizontal scheduling* allows for concurrent scheduling in several rooms, with the expectation that all rooms will be filled with sufficient volume to achieve high utilization.

Emerging Business Models in Anesthesia Services

The last item to cover before departing anesthesia services is the emerging business models for anesthesia practice groups. It has become increasingly difficult for historically small anesthesia practice groups to sustain both manpower and financial stability. Practice mergers are occurring at the local, national, and multistate level, and regional anesthesia practice groups are growing. Another emerging trend is for larger healthcare systems to offer employment options to physicians, including anesthesiologists.

Many new graduates of anesthesia programs are seeking employment models that reflect better work-life balance. Independent anesthesia practice groups have structured on-call coverage expectations in which newer, or junior, partner practitioners take heavier loads than senior practitioners. A similar disparity occurs with compensation and equity offers to newer practitioners. This has begun to create barriers to attracting new anesthesiologists to older, established practices.

At the same time, smaller groups are experiencing challenges with contracting, managing charge capture, billing, and collections. The anesthesia income model is one of the last payment models to follow adjusted time-based units. Many practices are now entering into alternative contracting models directly with payers and in partnership with other practice groups or hospitals in a bundled payment model.

These smaller groups have already been outsourcing these back-office processes and are struggling to keep up with the new payment models.

One alternative for small group practices is to merge and consolidate with other practices to gain scale and efficiency. However, these larger groups often serve multiple organizations in their geographic region. Healthcare organizations are identifying some risk in divulging strategic plans to their competitors.

Another alternative is to become acquired by larger regional and national anesthesia practices. In fact, several of these large groups offer more than just anesthesia services, including emergency department and radiology services. Healthcare organizations are being courted to consider this model, with turnkey programs promising reduced subsidies and improved performance while maintaining the highest quality outcomes. These larger organizations acquire the existing anesthesia practice, thereby keeping the same anesthesiologists engaged in providing care in the clinical areas.

The third alternative is for the healthcare organization to establish an employment program and set up, or contract for, business office operations. Table 7.1, later in the chapter, summarizes some of the pros and cons for healthcare organizations to consider in selecting the best anesthesia practice model.

CREATING SUCCESSFUL PARTNERSHIPS WITH SURGEONS

Surgeons are crucial partners to healthcare organizations, with the power to significantly impact the effective management of surgical services. With the proper guidance and information, surgeons can be instrumental in helping the organization achieve its strategic and operational goals. The surgical services executive needs to be proactive in planning interactions and establishing close working relationships. Surgeons frequently say they have never met, or rarely see, the surgical services vice president; therefore, they often carry their complaints and requests directly to the organization's CEO or COO.

The first tier of surgeon complaints is often narrow, with a focus on optimal case scheduling, achieving high levels of efficiency with nominal delays, and having the right team and resources to perform surgeries. These functions are extremely important to a surgeon's practice and should never be ignored. Tactics to accomplish these top concerns have been covered in detail in previous chapters of this book. This section of the chapter will provide background information about surgeon practices, functions of the medical staff's department of surgery, and helpful hints in managing the relationship between surgeons and the surgical services leadership team.

A Short Primer on Surgeon Practices

As you plan to meet and work with surgeons, maintain an awareness of what a physician practice is like today. Surgeons face numerous challenges in managing a successful practice. Similar to healthcare organizations, they must adapt to national healthcare policy changes. In *Medical Economics*, authors Terry, Ritchie, Marbury, Smith, and Pofeldt (2014) summarized the top six medical practice concerns:

1. Administrative burdens—including prior authorizations, coding, billing, and collections. Physicians are spending more time on their computers than attending to patients.

2. Independence versus secure employment is a constant pressure. Joining larger practices or hospital systems offers some

relief from these administrative burdens, but it comes with sacrifices to long-term compensation and independence.

3. Payers dictating healthcare, requiring extensive documentation for preauthorization, and submitting to a range of audits tied to meaningful use and other programs.

4. Patients dictating healthcare, becoming more involved in medical decisions, and requesting medications and treatment regimens that the physician may not deem necessary but feels pressured to provide to attain high patient satisfaction scores.

5. Staff retention—in their offices and on the hospital staff—to attain the highest levels of quality and efficiency (see Operating Room Nurse Practice Specialization in Chapter 6, "Nursing Management in Surgical Services").

6. Avoiding liability by practicing defensive medicine and staying current in evidence-based practice and innovations in surgical interventions.

In addition to managing a practice, surgeons may fill many roles within the organization. Typically, they have a professional commitment to participate in the medical staff organization and serve on hospital committees that support various functions in the hospital such as infection prevention and critical care committees. Departments of surgery have officers who are appointed to provide oversight of direction for the various surgical specialties. Each of these roles has defined responsibilities that need to be reviewed and understood to navigate within the surgical services department.

The department also will have several standing committees such as credentialing, peer review, or ongoing professional practice review. Reviewing the bylaws of both the medical staff and the department of surgery is a good way to learn more about surgeons' work. It can be helpful to map out the key physician leaders for easy and quick reference when you need medical staff support.

Another important preparation step is to understand the various models of surgical practice that you will encounter. Examples are provided in Table 7.1, though you may also see hybrids.

TABLE 7.1: SURGICAL PRACTICE MODELS

Surgical Practice Model	Description
Private practice	One or more surgeons have formed a business focused on a surgical specialty, with each having subspecialized
	Most common model in small to mid-size hospitals
Multispecialty group practice	Offers an array of surgical, medical, and other specialty services
	Most common form in practices working with a health system or multiple hospitals in a region
Surgical Practice Model	Description
Private or group practice, employed as contractor to provide certain services	Often seen with healthcare organizations that want to align with a physician but avoid purchase of a practice
Academic group practices	Affiliated with a university's medical school

WORKING EFFECTIVELY WITH SURGEONS

These are some common challenges and helpful tips for achieving productive working relationships with the surgical team:

Working with the angry surgeon

- Listen attentively.
- Do not jump to conclusions or confront with questions; the surgeon is not looking for the answer at that particular moment.
- Provide the surgeon with assurance and a promise to follow up.
- Participate in surgical service department rounds. The best time to do this is in the morning prior to start of surgery.
- Keep rounds brief—no more than five minutes. These quick check-ins reinforce your commitment to surgeon feedback and help identify any issue that might require a need for a follow-up meeting.
- Maintain visibility in the surgical department. This will allow you to observe, ask brief questions, and recognize the surgeons' contributions.

Stopping in the surgeon lounge

- Stop by periodically to get to know the surgeons.
- Briefly greet the surgeons, and stay if invited.
- Take the opportunity to provide short follow-up statements; hold on detailed explanations. Offer to talk more later.

Setting up meetings

- Hold an initial introductory meeting to establish the relationship and identify top priorities.
- Ask about good times to follow up; some prefer to touch base in the OR, others to meet in their office.
- Issue brief recap emails, but do not expect a response.

Confirm preferred methods of communication

- Keep emails brief; they might not be read, especially if they're lengthy or include attachments.
- Leave short voicemails.
- Post announcements or newsletters in locker rooms, lounges, and on bulletin boards at the OR control desk.

Discussing data and other reports

- Be prepared for challenges to data integrity because there is always suspicion on how data is reported or captured.
- Enlist surgeons in interpretation of data.

Physicians' disruptive behavior

- Acknowledge it and its impact to safe patient care.
- Clearly state that the behavior will be reviewed.
- Follow the policies and guidelines established by the medical staff.
- Follow up and maintain integrity.
- Be honest; admit to not knowing something.
- Follow up.
- Be transparent.

EXECUTIVE LEADERSHIP LESSONS

- Changes in federal healthcare policies as well as environmental challenges are some of the drivers of strained relationships between physicians and hospitals. There are a number of emerging models, however, that are better aligning performance incentives.

- Years of physician education and clinical training have focused on developing diagnostic and technical expertise as well as the confidence to practice autonomously. Physician practice emphasizes clinical problem-solving and implementing decisions in immediate or short timeframes. Few physicians have received training in management processes. This has led to frustration on the part of the physician, who simply wants the best care for the patient with as little fuss as possible in the surgical setting. The good news is that the management process closely resembles the clinical diagnostic and treatment process.

- Thoughtful and consistent communication is key to getting started with physicians in surgical services, including: understanding their goals, communicating the strategic objectives of the organization, and fixing operational issues that impede their practice.

- The majority of organizations continue to work with the same anesthesia practice group for years. Often contracts are renewed with little if any modifications to reflect the changing dynamics of managing surgical services. The best practice for contract review is to conduct meetings with group leaders to discuss what needs to be covered in the contract and gain consensus before engaging legal support.

- An anesthesia services coverage plan should reflect OR resource hours contained in the surgical services scheduling guidelines, specifically the number of OR suites or procedure rooms that are opened and staffed to meet surgeon case schedule demand. They may vary by day and by hour during the course of the day. Coverage for nonelective cases and on-call demand should also be addressed in the overall anesthesia coverage plan.

- Elective resource hours are staffed either with an anesthesiologist or with a certified registered nurse anesthetist (CRNA) under the supervision of an anesthesiologist. Exceptions may be found in those states that allow for a CRNA to administer anesthesia under the supervision of the surgeon.

- The anesthesia practice model is determined by the medical staff based on complexities of patient care for their organization. The practice model chosen also is dependent on the market availability of anesthesiologists and CRNAs.

- Keep in mind that anesthesia provides sedation and pain relief services in areas outside of the OR, including OB, pain management clinics, cardiology, etc. When budgeting staffing, these case volumes must be considered.

- Key anesthesia leadership roles and responsibilities need to be defined in the contract along with any compensation to be paid to the anesthesia group for these activities. Typically the roles include an anesthesia department chairperson or chief, anesthesia medical director, and chief CRNA. The requirement and responsibilities for the department chair or chief are found in the medical staff organization's bylaws.

- The Medical Group Management Association (MGMA) estimates that 85% of all hospitals subsidize the anesthesia groups in some way, with the typical range of $100,000–$150,000 per anesthetizing location, per year (MGMA, n.d.).

- The methods for establishing the subsidy are variable; the most common is based on a utilization model where a portion of the subsidy is paid when anesthesia coverage sites have a utilization or billable volume of below 70%.

- The anesthesia income model is one of the last payment models to follow adjusted time-based units. Many practices are now entering into alternative contracting models directly with payers and in partnership with other practice groups or hospitals in a bundled payment model.

- Surgeons frequently say they have never met, or rarely see, the surgical services vice president. Therefore, they often carry their complaints and requests directly to the organization's CEO or COO.

REFERENCES

Clark, M. (2013, September 11). *Our top resources on strengthening hospital-physician alignment* [Web log post]. Retrieved from https://www.advisory.com/research/care-transformation-center/care-transformation-center-blog/2013/09/accountable-for-progress-physician

Merlino, J. (2015, August 19). *The responsibility matrix: A strategy for stronger physician/administrator partnerships.* Retrieved from https://www.beckershospitalreview.com/hospital-physician-relationships

Metzner, J., & Domino, K. B. (2010). Risks of anesthesia or sedation outside the operating room: The role of the anesthesia care provider. *Current Opinion in Anesthesiology, 23,* 523–531.

MGMA. (n.d.). MGMA DataDive Cost and Revenue Data. https://www.mgma.com/data/benchmarking-data/costs-revenue-data

Terry, K., Ritchie, A., Marbury, D., Smith, L., & Pofeldt, E. (2014, December 1). Top 6 practice management challenges facing physicians in 2015: Physicians still face mountains of red tape in the upcoming year. *Medical Economics.* Retrieved from http://medicaleconomics.modernmedicine.com/medical-economics/news/top-6-practice-management-challenges-facing-physicians-2015?page=full

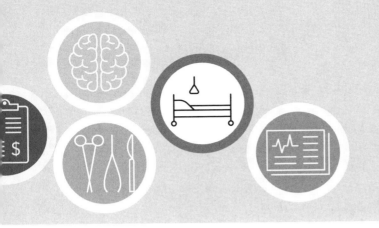

MEDICAL TOURISM

—Maggie Ozan-Rafferty, RN, MHA, MBA, DHA
Chief Experience Officer of Blessing Health System,
Quincy, Illinois

CASE STUDY

Mary Frye, the surgical services product line leader for a large Midwestern health-care system, was concerned. Over the past 8 months, she had seen a significant decrease in the number of arthroplasty and other surgeries in many of her hospitals. She had led the surgical services team for more than 12 years and, up until several months ago, had been very proud of the growth she had championed during her tenure—a 25% increase in the number of high-margin cases and dramatic improvements in quality and service.

Mary had worked very hard to develop relationships with surgeons across the system. She had leveraged her knowledge of physician preferences to create a surgeon-friendly environment; her operating suites had become the place where most local physicians wanted to bring their patients. She applied the same approach to her staff, recruiting experienced surgical nurses and assistants as well as creating an internal academy to train nonsurgical nurses in a 6-month training course taught onsite.

Knowing the national shortage of experienced surgical services staff was increasing, Mary and her leadership team met regularly with all members of the surgery team to ensure open lines of communication. They leveraged daily huddles, one-on-one personal meetings, and daily employee and surgeon rounds to enhance two-way feedback. Mary regularly monitored responses from formal and informal physician and employee surveys, taking steps to make improvements. Her survey results were in the top quartile nationally.

Quality measures in Mary's surgical services departments also were at or above the 10th percentile nationally. Improvements in infection rates, on-time starts, block-time utilization, and many other key measures became a real sense of pride for the surgical services team. Hospital administration regularly provided recognition in the form of department celebrations to acknowledge the accomplishments of the surgical services team.

Mary believed she and her team had taken surgical services to the next level in quality and service and was perplexed with the recent significant loss of surgical volume. She collaborated with the system director of planning and the strategy team to take a deeper dive into the drivers of the volume loss. The analysis pointed to a loss of surgical volume from two sources: local ambulatory surgery centers (ASCs) and a hospital system halfway across the country. Mary and the hospital team were aware of the expanded role of ASCs and had been preparing for the impact of several new physician-owned centers. However, deeper analysis uncovered a new threat to their hospital-based surgical services—the loss of volume to domestic medical tourism, where patients hopped on a plane and obtained care across the country.

DOMESTIC MEDICAL TOURISM

Over centuries, patients have traveled for medical treatment—for example, taking trips to the Dead Sea for its healing properties. However, over the past 15 years there has been an increase in people traveling from industrialized countries to developing nations to seek high-quality healthcare at lower costs. This phenomenon is known as medical tourism. Although accurate estimates of the number of U.S. medical tourists have been difficult to obtain, some researchers have forecasted significant losses in the billions of dollars for the US as a result of outbound medical travel (Deloitte Center for Health Solutions, 2009).

Well-known providers including the Cleveland Clinic and Johns Hopkins have built facilities or partnered with local providers in countries in the Middle East and Europe to capture a broader international patient base. While U.S. patients have traveled to centers of excellence for procedures such as organ transplants, more recently several U.S. healthcare systems and some individual hospitals are developing domestic medical tourism strategies, driving volume to their organizations from across the nation (Hudson & Xiang, 2012; Fotter, Malvery, Asi, Kirchner, & Warren, 2014).

Over the past decade, *bundled payment* (the packaging of an episode of patient care including tests, procedures, implants, drugs, durable medical equipment, professional fees, and services for a procedure such as joint replacement) has been championed by Medicare. However, there are a number of patients who explore lower-cost medical care within the US, and more companies have created arrangements to encourage employees to travel out of state for healthcare.

More recently, several large employers have negotiated with selected providers across the country to purchase bundled care for their employees (Slotkin, Ross, Coleman, & Ryu, 2017). Noting the variance in charges and outcomes across providers, the impetus for these large employers is to reduce the cost of care and improve quality for their employees. Typical arrangements between large companies and meticulously selected providers include full coverage for medical and travel expenses at a preset bundled rate and limited, or no, out-of-pocket cost for the employees. To participate in these arrangements, providers undergo an extensive review, which includes organizational and physician performance metrics such as infection rates, length of stay, return-to-work times, and postoperative outcomes. In addition to a metric analysis, providers undergo a site visit much like a Joint Commission review, which consists of a tracer of the patient's experience from initial contact to return to work and follow-up care. Once the review is complete, negotiation and contracting commence. In these models, while total reimbursement may be lower, the potential base of patients is significant, making domestic medical toursim an attractive option for hospitals and health systems (Anonymous, 2011; Slotkin et al., 2017).

The home improvement giant Lowe's, along with other large employers including Walmart, McKesson, and JetBlue Airways (among others), has partnered to help evaluate quality providers and negotiate bundled payments. These domestic medical travel arrangements include medical treatment for the employee as well as coverage for the cost of a caregiver to accompany the patient. For Lowe's, this has led to reduced employee out-of-pocket costs and high rates of patient satisfaction. Lowe's employees participating in the program also needed significantly less postoperative skilled nursing facility care and had low readmissions rates. The goal—better outcomes and cost savings—represents a win-win for both employees and employers (Anonymous, 2011; Slotkin et al., 2017).

Push Factors

Several dynamics are driving companies and employees to seek non-local providers for healthcare. As copays, deductibles, and the cost of insurance premiums have increased, patients have become more aware of their out-of-pocket costs, and many have become more comfortable with traveling for care that may cost less. Significant variation in pricing locally and nationally for key procedures such as joint replacements also has contributed to consumer and employer quests for better value, even if it means getting on a plane.

Tranparency and variance in quality outcomes such as readmission rates and surgical site infections also have created an environment in which consumers and employers are seeking providers with the highest quality (Carabello, 2015).

To encourage employees to participate in domestic medical tourism, some employers are waiving copays and deductibles and including travel and nonhospital accommodations for both the employee and a caregiver.

Pull Factors

Organizations seeking to attract domestic medical tourists have several attributes that merit their selection as providers. Premier organizations such as the Cleveland Clinic have an existing high-quality brand, and in the Clinic's case, all members of the medical staff are hospital employees, which makes it easier to establish prices. Geisinger Health System became a destination care provider for domestic medical travelers after implementing several extensive process-improvement initiatives to enhance workflow. They also incorporated additional error-proofing approaches to minimize variation and improve patient touchpoints.

Risks

There are risks associated with traveling for medical care. For instance, flying may increase the risk of blood clots, and local physicians may be reluctant to provide care for complications on another physician's patient.

While employees may be offered a choice of providers, they may feel pressured to travel or be upset that they are away from other family members, resulting in the typical issues associated with disgruntled employees. If insurers and providers focus solely on costs and not quality, then patient care will be affected.

Long-Term Outlook

With globalization, ease of travel and communication, as well as evolving tele-health capability, the market for healthcare services is likely to expand as long as patients, employers, and payers demand high-quality care at the best prices.

In a 2009 study by the Deloitte Center for Health Solutions, more than 40% of U.S. patients said they would be willing to travel away from their immediate area if their physician recommended it or if they could achieve a 50% cost savings. The hope is that domestic medical tourism may force hospitals to focus on quality and efficiency and drive a new level of competition as organizations strive to be preferred providers.

Hospitals, health systems, and even some cities and states are hoping to brand themselves as destination healthcare providers. The Texas Medical Center in Houston is home to some of the nation's top hospitals and has positioned itself as a provider of specialty treatments with high-quality outcomes. Mayo Clinic, Johns Hopkins, and Baptist Health System have marketing initiatives that target both national and international patients. In a study on medical tourism by the Maricopa Association of Governments, the state of Arizona is evaluating how to leverage its amenities and over 300 days of sunshine to attract patients, while acknowledging that it has only one nationally recognized subspecialty provider (Barrow Neurological Institute) and limited collaboration between its state and local governments, the medical schools, and hospitals (Chantarakarn, Foley, James, & Pandey, 2014).

ASCs POSE AN ADDITIONAL THREAT

In addition to the loss of volume from domestic medical tourism, surgical services leaders are facing a shift away from hospital-based procedures to the outpatient setting. Nowhere has this been more apparent than the shift from inpatient surgeries to ambulatory surgical centers (ASCs) and particularly for joint replacement procedures.

Clinical advances in anesthesia, surgical techniques (such as smaller incisions), and pain management, coupled with changes in reimbursement, are resulting in some surgeons moving their total joint procedures to the outpatient setting where lengths of stay may be less than 23 hours. Because joint replacement surgeries are often one of the most profitable product lines, the loss of these surgeries poses a significant threat to hospital finances. Typically, healthy patients are candidates for outpatient joint surgeries, leaving patients with expensive comorbidities or unstable conditions in the inpatient setting.

In addtion, shifts in ambulatory reimbursement by Medicare may see a more significant number of joint replacements completed on an outpatient basis. As consumers are paying a larger portion of their healthcare costs, health systems are also experiencing a push to reduce out-of-pocket costs via more cost-effective ambulatory settings. Nevada, Illinois, and Colorado are among the states that have laws allowing patients to recover in an ASC for more than 72 hours. Other states, including Florida and Oregon, are examining bills for extended recovery care. United Healthcare announced in October 2016 that it will not allow designated outpatient surgery procedures to be performed in the hospital outpatient department without authorization (Meyer, 2016).

IMPLICATIONS FOR SURGICAL SERVICES LEADERSHIP

The move from volume to value is mandating that healthcare leaders realize that "what got them here won't get them there." It starts with ensuring that surgical services and all support departments are running as efficiently as possible and delivering high-quality outcomes and exceptional patient experiences.

Process-improvement initiatives—such as ensuring ease of registration and parking, reducing the number of patients who receive a blood transfusion, encouraging early mobility after surgery, and providing physical therapy the same day of surgery—are key intiatives to ensure high-quality outcomes. For joint and other elective patients, extensive presurgical education and support via classes and online programs can help to improve recovery time and reduce complications. Creating a combined inpatient and ambulatory joint program may be an attractive option for payers and providers (Kennedy & Kehayes, 2017).

Hunkering down and thinking "this too shall pass" by relying on traditional relationships and fighting the move to ASCs is a recipe for failure. Waiting until the risk of losing volume to an ASC is imminent may impact an organization's ability to build core expertise in ambulatory surgery. By actively seeking partners and creating a dedicated ASC management structure, there may be some short-term financial pain from the loss of inpatient volume. However, this option provides positioning for the organization as it moves into a value-based health-care environment (Kennedy & Kehayes, 2017).

MOVING TO A VALUE-BASED HEALTHCARE ENVIRONMENT

- Create an environment of ownership and high employee and physician engagement, where staff feel empowered to deliver exceptional care and work collaboratively with providers.

- Increase efficiency of block time utiltization and facilitate turnover-time reductions, while ensuring that on-time starts are the rule; this will enable surgeons to be more productive and, ideally, to increase their case volumes.

- Create a simplified automated scheduling system that is collaborative with the surgeon's office representatives, reducing the amount of time to schedule procedures and helping to eliminate scheduling errors.

- Dedicate time and resources to the preadmission testing area (PAT), which is often the first impression a patient has of an organization. This can help to ensure on-time starts, prevent case cancellations, decrease delays, and properly prepare patients to reduce complications and readmissions (Becker's Hospital Review, 2016).

- Share data regarding on-time starts, turnover time, outcomes, etc., and celebrate improvements in key goals and milestones with physicians and staff.

- Ensure collaboration between hospitals and surgeons to deliver the best care in the best environment. Explore shared ownership of ASCs.

- Revisit hospital outpatient surgery department pricing to align with those of ASCs or assume case will be taken (when possible) to an ASC.

- Create a willingness to contract with out-of-state employers and insurers for services at a bundled or discounted price, while ensuring new contracts do not jeopardize existing contracts.

- Collaborate with local chambers of commerce, corporations, and other healthcare facilities to market the competitive advantage of the hospital, health system, or local providers.

These are very challenging times for healthcare administrators and, particularly, for surgical services leaders faced with multiple threats to their core business. The recent deals among nontraditional providers such as CVS and Aetna are about to change the ways Americans receive medical care, shifting away from hospitals and emergency departments and toward clinics, physician offices, ASCs, and even the local drugstore (Mathews & Evans, 2017).

Failure to adapt to new and emerging models of care in a value versus volume environment will result in consolidation or closure of service lines as payers and patients insist that care be provided in the right place, at the right time, for the right reasons, and for the right cost. Disruptive innovators are emerging from unlikely sources in healthcare, and this is an exciting time to be driving organizational change. Hold on to your surgical bonnet, be part of the solution, and enjoy the ride!

EXECUTIVE LEADERSHIP LESSONS

- Executives need to expand their operating definition of competition to reflect the trends in both global and domestic medical tourism, as well as threats from non-traditional providers and sites of care.

- Although government payers have backed away from mandated bundle payments for now, the concept is not going away. In a value-based payment environment, insurers, employers, and consumers themselves are contracting for services based on cost, convenience, and clinical outcomes.

- Becoming a healthcare destination requires close partnership with state and local governments, insurers, your local business community including chambers of commerce, physicians, and your executive leadership team.

- In an effort to stay competitive, you will need to measure and monitor consumer-oriented performance metrics focused on convenience, ease of access, and service.

- As you look to improve internal surgical service processes, keep in mind that employers and consumers are requiring a reduction in process/system variation and an intensification of data transparency.

- Focus continual improvement efforts on consumer-oriented processes such as access, parking, registration, turn-around times, follow-up contacts, etc.

REFERENCES

Anonymous. (2011, October). Domestic medical travel programs aim to improve results, cut costs. *IOMA's Report on Managing Benefits Plans, 13*(10), p. 16.

Becker's Hospital Review. (2016, June 21). How to align surgeons to increase productivity and curtail outmigration. *Becker's Hospital Review*. Retrieved from https://www.beckershospitalreview.com/hospital-physician-relationships/how-to-align-surgeons-to-increase-productivity-and-curtail-outmigration.html

Carabello, L. (2015, August 17). Domestic medical travel: What HR should know: A key driver is the demand for cost-effective, high-quality outpatient surgeries. *HRNews*. Retrieved from http://ezproxy.library.unlv.edu/login?url=https://search.proquest.com/docview/1704359184?accountid=3611

Chantarakarn, C., Foley, S., James, W., & Pandey, R. (2014). *Medical toursim in Arizona.* Maricopa Association of Governments. Retrieved from http://www.azmag.gov/Portals/0/Documents/EDC_2013-12-03_Medical-Tourism-in-Arizona-Final-Report.pdf

Deloitte Center for Health Solutions. (2009). *Medical tourism: Update and implications.* Retrieved from http://www.coa.org/docs/DeloitteStudyMedicalTourism_111209_web.pdf

Fotter, M. D., Malvery, D., Asi, Y., Kirchner, S., & Warren, N. A. (2014). Can inbound and domestic medical tourism improve your bottom line? Identifying the potential of a U.S. tourism market. *Journal of Healthcare Management, 59*(1), 49–63. Retrieved from https://journals.lww.com/jhmonline/Fulltext/2014/01000/Can_Inbound_and_Domestic_Medical_Tourism_Improve.9.aspx

Hudson, S., & Xiang, L. (2012). Domestic medical tourism: A neglected dimension of medical tourism research. *Journal of Hospitality Marketing & Management, 21*(3), 227–246. doi: 10.1080/19368623.2011.615018

Kennedy, K., & Kehayes, I. N. (2017, October). *ASCs at a tipping point: The new reality of surgical services for health systems.* Paper presented at Health System 100, Amelia Island, FL. Retrieved from https://www.healthsystem100.com/application/files/8615/0420/6320/ASCs_at_a_Tipping_Point_-_Whitepaper.pdf

Mathews, J. W., & Evans, M. (2017, December 20). Flurry of health-care deals reflects shift away from hospitals. *The Wall Street Journal.* Retrieved from https://www.wsj.com/articles/as-medical-care-shifts-out-of-hospitals-companies-plan-deals-1513716507?mod=searchresults&page=1&pos=17

Meyer, H. (2016, June 4). Replacing joints faster, cheaper and better? *Modern Healthcare.* Retrieved from http://www.modernhealthcare.com/article/20160604/MAGAZINE/306049986

Slotkin, J. R., Ross, O. A., Coleman, R., & Ryu, J. (2017, June 8). Why GE, Boeing, Lowes and Walmart are directly buying health care for employees. *Harvard Business Review.* Retrieved from https://hbr.org/2017/06/why-ge-boeing-lowes-and-walmart-are-directly-buying-health-care-for-employees

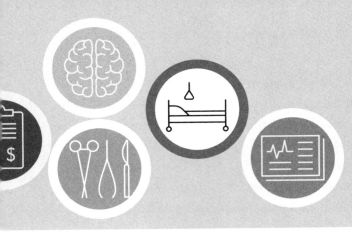

AFTERWORD

A literature search of current issues affecting surgical services management produces a mind-boggling array of topics, including such disparate concerns as *the optimal preoperative assessment of the geriatric patient, improvement in surgical instrumentation safety, scientific findings in block time scheduling,* and *enhanced recovery clinical pathway implementation.* This search doesn't even include contemporary issues related to risk management, bundled payments for surgical care, surgeon-hospital partnerships, and competition against or partnerships with for-profit ambulatory centers.

It's no wonder an experienced hospital executive recently shared this account:

> *The OR scared me when I was new in my role. I knew every other area of the hospital except the OR. They spoke a foreign language as far as I was concerned. But I knew the stakes were high. It drove a huge percentage of our revenue, and the surgeons always seemed unhappy about something. I had no choice but to abdicate decision-making to the OR Committee, even though they reported to the Medical Executive Committee and not me. Early in my career, I didn't know another way to do it. This worried me, however, because surgical services came up at every board meeting. A big portion of our strategic plan was tied to revenue growth in the OR.*

Surely this executive is not unique in feeling a bit overwhelmed with management of surgical services, where the stakes are indeed high. In fact, the very definition of the traditional operating room (OR) evolves each year as technology advancements such as hybrid suites blur the lines among surgery, radiology, and cardiology. The challenge for the new executive is that our current systems and processes were created during an era when boundaries among specialties were well defined, and shared, interdisciplinary decision-making was virtually nonexistent. Nurses managed nurses, supplies, and procedures. Surgeons, as "captains of the ship," directed clinical care, often with a singular (and not infrequently self-serving) perspective. Priorities were often misaligned, and the fee-for-service payer model placed hospitals and physicians at odds.

Then the world shifted. Disruptive payer models drove us to unheard-of partnerships, personal preferences for equipment could no longer be accommodated as cost pressures drove standardization, and catastrophic errors could best be avoided by looking to the airline industry for guidance. Standardized "preflight" checklists have been adapted to surgery and have inextricably altered our surgical world, and most surgical "ship captains" now recognize the importance of shipmate perspectives. Trends in employee empowerment challenged the traditional power structure, and large, investor-owned surgical management groups entered the scene.

Every aspect of surgical services management will continue to be challenged. Consumers will demand service levels they have come to expect in retail. Employers, hefting a huge percentage of the healthcare tab, will negotiate directly with hospitals, irrespective of location, for these costly services. Clinical outcomes, including eradication of complications and untoward events, will become the challenge for clinical leaders. Though the environment is complex, executives can make a significant contribution in the leadership of surgical services for the benefit of patients and clinicians alike.

We hope this book has shortened your learning curve. Though the landscape is changing rapidly, having a set of tools—including tried and tested organizational charts, job descriptions, performance metrics, and team charters—can reduce decision-cycle time. While complex and challenging, surgical services does not have to be difficult or scary to lead. In perhaps no other area of a hospital are the opportunities as great for partnership, shared decision-making, and innovative business models.

–Gerald E. Biala
Therese A. Fitzpatrick

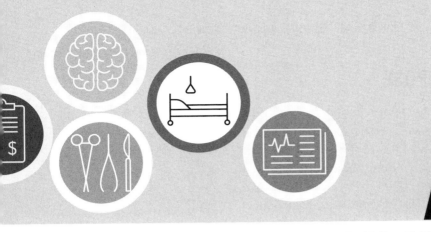

A

SCHEDULING GUIDELINES FOR SURGERY

PURPOSE

These guidelines have been established to support (*insert hospital name*) in achieving strategic goals and operational objectives.

Foremost among these objectives are to:

- Increase patient satisfaction
- Increase surgeon satisfaction
- Achieve fiscal responsibilities

The Perioperative Executive Council (PEC) has developed and approved these guidelines and will make amendments as needed.

These guidelines serve as the principles by which patients are scheduled for surgery, and surgical services resources are managed.

The nursing department and anesthesia department will be responsible for following these guidelines in day-to-day schedule management decisions.

Surgeons may request changes to be made to these guidelines through the PEC Chair.

1. SETTING THE UTILIZATION TARGET

1.1. Sufficient operating rooms and hours will be opened and staffed to meet the demand for elective, emergency, and urgent cases and a targeted utilization rate based on the strategic and operational objectives of (*insert hospital name*). Current rooms and hours open, along with a targeted utilization rate, are listed in Addendum 1.

1.1.1. Overall OR utilization will be monitored monthly and adjusted quarterly to meet demand.

1.1.2. Decision to close a room is based on the absence of or insufficient number of cases to fill a room for at least 4 hours of surgery.

1.1.3. Decision to close a room will not automatically call for a decrease in staffing or affect the ability to place add-on or emergency cases to the schedule. Likewise, decisions will also take into account the need to flex staff up for cases.

1.1.4. A preliminary decision to close a room can be considered as much as 1 week in advance, allowing time for the scheduling office to verify with surgeon(s) offices about the absence of scheduled cases or the options to consolidate cases within OR suites. The decision will be affirmed during the huddle and finalized at no later than 1400 on the day before surgery.

1.1.4. Ongoing monitoring and review will occur to ensure the intent of this procedure is met and quality standards are maintained. The PEC will review this data regularly to ensure utilization meets demand.

2. ASSIGNING CASE TIMES

2.1. Elective cases are scheduled to start in a room at the opening hours at 0730 on Mondays, Wednesdays, Thursdays, and Fridays and at 0815 on Tuesdays. Following PEC approval, some designated rooms may start later for surgeons with early-morning academic commitments.

2.1.1. Estimated length of cases is based on the OR information system historic calculation or if the surgeon requests a longer case time.

2.1.2. Start time on the schedule means the time the patient enters the operating room.

2.1.3. The surgeon should be present in the hospital at least 15 minutes prior to scheduled start time.

2.1.4. For multiple procedure cases, the surgeon beginning the case must be available at the start time of the case.

2.1.5. Cases scheduled for start times after the opening hours (not a first case start) are subject to being moved later if the schedule warrants.

2.1.5.1. The surgeon will be contacted and offered the opportunity to move the case time up before adjusting the start time.

3. BLOCK TIME ALLOCATION

3.1. The PEC is responsible for the allocation of surgical time based on historical data, strategic goals, and equity between surgical specialties. Blocks of time are distributed to surgical specialties and individual physicians.

3.2. Section chairs are responsible for determining how block time will be distributed in their respective specialties following the direction of the PEC regarding targets of utilization. Changes of the allocations within their specialties are recommended to the PEC. The following facts should be considered:

- Surgeon historical utilization

- Program growth

- New surgeons' needs

- Resource needs in the surgical suite

4. BLOCK TIME UTILIZATION

4.1. Block time utilization is calculated by:

(Case Time + Turnover) / (Allocated time) = Utilization

4.1.1. Block time utilization will be monitored monthly and adjusted as needed to meet targets. The PEC will formally review on a semi-annual basis.

4.1.2. Surgical and turnover time adjacent to the allocated block time will be used for the calculation of the utilization.

4.1.3. Surgical and turnover time used outside of the block time will be reported as total time out of block.

4.1.4. Assigned blocks may be released by the specialty or surgeon by notice to the OR scheduling office but will remain part of the block utilization calculation.

4.1.5. A separate monitor for released blocked time will be maintained if blocks are repeatedly released (if affecting the block utilization assigned).

4.1.6. Other aspects considered in the review of block utilization will include:

- Chronic lateness

- Overbooking

- Booking phantom patients to hold block time

- Chronic cancellation of cases

- Chronic release of block time 7 business days in advance

- Nonpreventable cancellations

4.1.7. Block time will be first released to the specialty service per the table below. If not used by the services, it will be released to all surgeons on a first come, first serve basis.

4.1.8. Requests for block or additional block time are made in writing and submitted to the specialty chairman and brought to the PEC for consideration. A block time recommendation is made to the PEC.

5. RELEASE OF BLOCK TIME

5.1. Block time will be released as follows:

Service	Surgeon	To Open Time
Orthopedics	*7 days	2 days
Plastics	*14 days	2 days
ENT	*14 days	2 days
Oral	*14 days	4 days
Ophthalmology	*5 days	4 days
GU	*7 days	2 days
Hand	*3 days	2 days
General	*7 days	2 days
Vascular	1 day	11 a.m. day prior
Cardiac	1 day	11 a.m. day prior
Thoracic	1 day	11 a.m. day prior
Neurosurgery	1 day	11 a.m. day prior

6. SCHEDULE CLOSE

6.1. The surgical schedule will close at 1300 for elective cases on the workday prior to the scheduled day of surgery. Any case scheduled after this time will be considered an add-on, and start times cannot be guaranteed.

7. OPEN TIME

7.1. Open time will be allocated on a first come, first serve basis, given the following conditions:

- Surgeons who do not have allocated block time

- Surgeons who have used or released all other block time within the week

- For use as needed by all surgeons to meet demand

8. SCHEDULING OF CASES

8.1. Scheduling *inside* of your surgical priority time

8.1.1. To schedule a surgical case in your block time, use (insert IT system name) email to (inset) or fax your reservation form to (insert).

8.1.2. Surgeon may call scheduling office (insert) to schedule a case, but written confirmation as above should follow.

8.1.3. All cases scheduled will receive a faxed confirmation the following day. Surgeons' offices are responsible for ensuring that cases are confirmed through this method.

8.2. Scheduling *outside* your surgical block time or if you have *no* block time

8.2.1. To schedule a surgical case *outside* your assigned block time, contact the surgical scheduling office by calling (*insert*). If time is available on the preferred day, surgical scheduling will immediately confirm the request. If time is not available on the preferred day, open time on alternate dates will be offered.

8.2.2. If the above process does not result in satisfactory date and time for your operation, the office may request the case be placed on a waiting list for block time released by other services. Cases scheduled in wait rooms cannot be approved until block time is released by other services. This may occur between 1 and 5 days prior to requested date.

8.3. Scheduling of elective cases

8.3.1. No elective cases shall be scheduled without the following patient information: patient's legal name, birth date, sex, address (including city and zip code), phone number, alternative phone (if available), pre-op diagnosis, primary and any secondary procedures with laterality or level if applicable, referring and consulting physicians, admission status, implants required, who supplies implants, patient's allergies, any history of infectious diseases or latex allergy, MRSA or VRE status, type of anesthesia, any special requests (e.g., c-arm, laser, etc.), and name of the individual scheduling the procedure.

8.3.2. If the above information is not available at the time of scheduling, the physician's office should call back with the appropriate information as soon as possible. The scheduling office will try to help track the missing demographic information through the hospital medical records. If the information is not available, the scheduling office will notify the surgeon's office and make all attempts to gain this information before canceling the case.

8.3.3. Accurate boarding of the actual procedure(s) is critically important.

8.3.4. Requests for hospital-provided surgical assistants must be made by the surgeon at the time of scheduling.

8.3.5. If two or more surgeons are to operate on the same patient, all surgeons will be listed at the time of boarding. Information on the working order of the surgeons is needed at this time also. The surgeon who has scheduled the case should be the one arriving to do the case, as supplies are pulled on a per-case-per-surgeon basis.

8.3.6. When scheduling total joint replacements, open reduction and internal fixations (ORIFs), or other procedures that may require an implant, the physician's office should identify the type of implant that the physician plans on using and include it as part of the procedure.

8.3.7. When scheduling a case that requires the use of X-ray imaging, identify that need as part of the procedure. Only *three* fluoroscopy cases can be scheduled at a time due to radiology technician coverage.

8.3.8. For those scheduled procedures that involve anatomical sites that have laterality, the word(s) *right*, *left*, or *bilateral* will be written out fully on the procedure/operating room schedule and on all relevant documentation (e.g., consents).

8.3.9. Any discrepancies in data will be clarified with the physician's office.

In instances where the anatomical site cannot be confirmed due to the patient's clinical condition, STBD (side(s)/site(s) to be determined) will be entered on the schedule

8.4. Scheduling of add-ons and emergency cases

8.4.1. Add-ons and emergency cases for the next day are scheduled as follows:

- If before 1700 on the day prior to the surgical date, contact the surgical scheduling office by phone (*insert*) or stop by the scheduling office to schedule the case.

- If after 1700 on the day prior to the surgical date, contact the OR charge nurse at (*insert*).

9. MANAGING ADD-ON CASES

9.1. Urgent and elective add-on cases will be done according to the order scheduled.

9.2. There may be exceptions based upon availability of resources for quality medical care, availability of equipment and instrumentation, or the mutual convenience of the OR and the operating surgeon.

9.3. Surgeons posting add-on cases shall be expected to work when a room becomes available.

9.4. If a surgeon is not available, the case is relisted on the add-on list at the discretion of the anesthesia and nursing coordinators.

9.5. If a surgeon is already present in the OR, attempts will be made to permit him/her to do add-on cases consecutively with scheduled cases, as long as it does not interfere with prior scheduled cases or prior add-on cases of other surgeons.

10. BUMPING GUIDELINES

10.1. A "bumped" case is defined as any scheduled surgical case that is delayed, for 30 minutes or more, by an emergency case. Upon identification of the need to perform an emergency surgical procedure, the surgeon or resident physician must notify the OR schedule team lead. During regular hours of operation, the

SMT will evaluate the availability of operating rooms and personnel, and the OR mediator may be called upon, as the final decision-maker if a question exists. The order in which emergency cases are scheduled, as well as the determination to bump a scheduled case, will depend on the seriousness of the patient's condition. The determination of whom to bump will be based on the following guidelines:

10.1.1. In cases of emergent cases where minutes make a difference, the first available room will be bumped.

10.1.1.1 Emergent eye cases include, but are not limited to: a decomposing eye, vision impairment that could progress to total loss of vision, a detached retina, and embedded foreign bodies.

10.1.2. If possible, the OR will have the bumping surgeon move one of his or her own scheduled cases. If other surgeons are scheduled to follow, they will be accommodated ahead of the "bumping" surgeon.

10.1.3. If the surgeon is not able to bump him- or herself, the bump will be within the same service (e.g., orthopedic trauma bumps orthopedic service).

10.1.4. If the service to be bumped has more then one room running, the surgeon in the service who was bumped last will not be bumped.

10.1.5. If an emergent case occurs at a time when bumping service is not operating, then the first available room will be bumped.

10.1.6. When more than one emergency case is pending, the decision as to which is more urgent will be made by the following:

10.1.6.1. During the normal workday: The SMT will confer with the OR Mediator to determine priority.

10.1.6.2. After hours and weekends: The on-call trauma surgeon in the medical center will determine the priority.

10.1.7. When an emergency case from the night before will result in a case delay, the elective case of the same service doing the emergency will be delayed.

10.1.8. A bump log will be kept in order to track bump frequency and surgeon/service impacted.

10.1.9. The SMT will refer to the bump list to assist in making bumping decisions.

10.1.10. If another case is delayed in order to facilitate the emergency procedure, the OR schedule team lead will facilitate the notification of the surgeon, patient, significant others, and all persons and departments affected by the change

10.1.11. If disputes arise, decisions will be made by the SMT and escalated to the OR mediator.

10.1.12. When a room is held for traumas, the OR nurse manager will confirm the status of the alert within 20 minutes.

11. SCHEDULING OF SWING ROOMS

11.1. Consideration for swinging a surgeon between two rooms will be made by the OR manager and anesthesiologist in charge if an open room is available (see Addendum 1). Cases will be monitored for compliance in meeting criteria. The following criteria will be used when considering swinging a surgeon:

11.1.1. Surgeons who work beyond 1500 hours and have elective cases scheduled to follow that exceed 6 hours of surgery time.

11.1.2. Swing rooms will be considered on a first come, first scheduled basis and whenever possible should be made at the huddle prior to the day of surgery.

11.1.3. Surgeons are expected to move between swing rooms with no delay.

11.1.4. For each swing room, there is a target of 60 minutes between the end of one case and the surgeon availability for the next case start time.

11.1.5. There should be no undue delay between when the patient enters the room and the incision time.

11.1.6. The surgeon, and all other members of the surgical team, will commit to remain immediately available to ensure efficiency of swinging rooms.

11.1.7. Sufficient staff, instruments, and equipment must be planned for and available.

11.1.8. Swinging of cases may follow other already boarded cases in the second room.

11.1.9. Anesthesia, nursing, and the surgeon will make the decision on swinging a surgeon's cases.

11.1.10. Bumping of swing rooms for emergency cases will occur following the bumping rules in this policy.

11.1.11. The continuance of swinging cases for a surgeon may not be available after 5:00 p.m. When necessary, this decision will be determined jointly by the surgeon, anesthesiology, and nurse coordinators.

SURGICAL SERVICES CASE SCHEDULING
Addendum 1:
Rooms and Hours Open

Targeted Utilization Mondays Through Fridays

■ Per IDPH (document #9826) (*insert hospital name*) is licensed to run at a maximum of xx total operating rooms not including ophthalmology.

■ The total number of operating rooms opened and staffed will be flexed based on a target utilization of 80%.

Rooms Opened

Day of Week	Time	Total Rooms[1]	Insert Site[2]	Insert 2nd Site[2]
Monday	0730–1500	12	10	6
Tuesday	0815–1500	12	10	6
Wednesday	0730–1500	12	10	6
Thursday	0730–1500	12	10	6
Friday	0730–1500	12	10	6
Monday–Friday	1500–1700	8	8	6
Monday–Friday	1700–2000	4	4	0
Monday–Friday	2000–2300	2	2	0
Monday–Friday	2300–0730	1	1	0
Saturday	0730–1500	1	1	0

[1]—Total of rooms to be opened and staffed across both sites (NOTE: Does not include swing rooms assigned to a single OR team)

[2]—Maximum number of rooms available

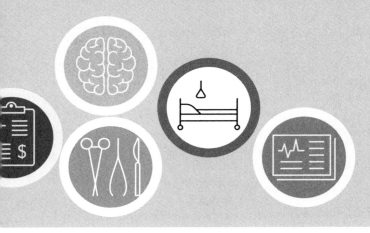

INDEX

B

C

N

O